From Pardon and Protest

From Pardon and Protest

memoirs from the margins

Una O'Higgins O'Malley

Arlen House
2001

first published in October   2001 by

Arlen House
PO Box 222
Galway

and

42 Grange Abbey Road
Baldoyle
Dublin 13
Ireland

ISBN:

1–903631–17–3 paperback
1–903631–18–1 hardback

www.arlenhouse.ie

Design by Dunleavy Design, Salthill, Galway
Printed by ColourBooks, Baldoyle, Dublin 13

CONTENTS

For the countless unknown people
who struggle to build peace
and whose names are not mentioned
in this or any other book

ACKNOWLEDGEMENTS

All the photographers, artists, archives and information repositories for the photos and paintings in this book, including the RTÉ Archives (the Cashman Collection) for the photograph of my parents, John Short for the painting of the grandchildren, Sean O'Sullivan RHA for the portraits of Maev and I, Derek Spiers and Report, the *Irish Times*, the *Evening Press,* Dermot O'Flynn, Jimmie Sheehan, and Jerry O'Gorman. The poem 'Just God' appeared in *Poetry Ireland Review* (Summer 2000), The poem 'A Widow's Child' appeared in *Jumping the Bus Queue* edited by Mary Rose Callaghan, The Older Women's Network/Age and Opportunity.

My warm thanks are due to the members of the Writers Group to which I have belonged for some years – especially to Anne Keough who first read my script. My neighbour Colleen Burns has been like a midwife in helping to bring it to the light of day. My husband Eoin has shared his home with it with generosity and with commitment. Without the endless patience of my son Finbarr my computer would have got the better of my sanity.

My sincere appreciation also is offered to the writers of the humbling endorsements, to Mary Robinson, Tim Pat Coogan, Dervla Murphy, Enda McDonagh and Sir Alan Goodison, to Garret FitzGerald and to Michael D. Higgins for helping send the book on its way, to the Royal College of Surgeons and the Irish Association, the Kenny family in Galway and Adrienne Anifant of Arlen House who helped speed the book to the printers in remarkable time.

But none of these thanks could have been offered had not my publisher, Alan Hayes of Arlen House, believed that this was a story worth telling and so to him is due my deepest gratitude.

(Our apologies to those whom we have forgotten to mention on this page – your help and support has not been forgotten in the creation of this book and in the philosophy of what this book represents).

FOREWORD (S)

Una O'Higgins O'Malley has dedicated her public life to the search for peace on the island of Ireland. Driven by the thoughts and writings of her father, Kevin O'Higgins, who was assassinated when she was 5 months old, Una was one of the founders of the Glencree Reconciliation Centre, instrumental in the establishment of the Glenstal Ecumenical Conference and is a former President of the Irish Association. Writing about her father Una said:

> ... I understand him facing daily on-the-ground realities, determined to deal with the here-and-now and not with the what might-have-been.

In describing Una's work and commitment I would use the same description, with an additional phrase:

> Una has faced daily on-the-ground realities, determined to deal with the here-and-now *and the what must be achieved* – and not with the what might-have-been.

Una's guiding lights have been the need for forgiveness and reconciliation and it is timely that her memoirs are published at this significant time for Northern Ireland, Britain and Ireland. Her story is an important element of our contemporary history.

Mary Robinson

The *Margins* of the subtitle are something of an understatement. As the daughter of Kevin O'Higgins, assassinated when she was five months old – and as the granddaughter of Dr Thomas Higgins, assassinated four years previously – Una inherited a place in Irish life less than central but certainly not marginal. She also inherited a challenge: how to react to the manner of her father's death? Political assassinations are unlike either crimeland murders or soldiers' deaths on a conventional battlefield. In a tiny country like Ireland their after-shocks can and do affect generations of relatives and factional supporters.

As Terence de Vere White observed in his biography of Kevin O'Higgins, 'A civil war breeds unnatural hatreds'. *From Pardon and Protest* records the author's struggle to combat those hatreds throughout a lifetime spanning almost the entire history of the Irish state.

These very personal memoirs are, between their unpretentious lines, quite dramatic. (And at times, inevitably contentious – even in the year 2001). In the beginning was the violent death of an unknown but subsequently hero-worshipped father. His vision of a united, independent Ireland under a dual monarchy (avoiding permanent partition by accepting the British monarch as head of state) profoundly influenced his younger daughter's attitude to Northern Unionists. This enabled her, from 1972 onwards, to help in the building of ecumenical bridges during the worst of the Northern conflict. These were small, frail bridges – but not insignificant. Ultimately they were used by certain key figures who, without them, might have found it much more difficult to reach the other side.

Dervla Murphy

Una O'Higgins O'Malley embodies in herself and expresses in this book some of the deepest political hurt and the most liberating forgiveness in Irish life in the twentieth century.

This book is a further contribution by her in helping us become a forgiven and a forgetting people – that is a Christian people.

Enda McDonagh

Inspired by the example of her father, Una O'Higgins O'Malley has devoted much of her life to the promotion of peace and understanding among the differing strands of opinion on the island of Ireland. She has thus come to know many of the principal figures of her time. I look forward to reading the memoirs of a poet who has lived in engagement with the world.

Sir Alan Goodison
British Ambassador to Dublin, 1983–86

Una Higgins O'Malley comes from a family closely associated with the triumphs and tragedies of the Irish Physical Force tradition. Her work in attempting to eradicate this tradition from Irish life is well-known. Although at the time of writing the peace-makers' efforts have temporarily (hopefully) grounded on the rocks of the inability of some Northern politicians to translate that ancient expression, 'Ulster Says No', into contemporary language, ie 'Ulster Says Yes', Una Higgins O'Malley, as her memoirs show, will always be able to reply with pride to that root situation question of the next generation 'What did you do in the war?'

She can say with truth and dignity: 'I tried'.

Read the book.

Tim Pat Coogan

from
Pardon
and
Protest

FROM PARDON AND FROM PROTEST

I am from heads held high, stiff upper lips
and "the Clan's" affectionate laughter
where the pain was seldom spoken to the children
– and never among the teacups.

I am from Celtic spirals and the unresolved riddles
of twisted serpents scrolled on holy pages
I am from dancing-class and make-believe
and graven plaque on cenotaph unheeded.

I am from motherhood and meetings
and an unrelenting trail of grocery trolleys;
I am from history and politics
and letters to the press and pictures of my father.

I am from lines of pilgrims thumbing beads
upon their journeys,
From surgeon's spattered vests and the near-certainty
of an all-loving Godhead
I am *from pardon and from protest* and – like the spirals
I return to where I came from.

INTRODUCTION

Having spent my early, most formative years in an all-female household reared by a mother whose own childhood had been, in that respect, largely similar, I have been slow to believe that the lives of women are any less important than those of men. When ploughing through Caesar's Gallic Wars, for example, or later gazing at portraits of distinguished doctors, let's say, or of starched Cardinals or Archbishops (whether in Rome or Lambeth Palace) my mind has invariably wandered to the women behind the men, the women who had made or laundered the lace surplices and lawn sleeves for the clergy, to the matrons and nursing-staff behind those doctors – not to mention the domestic staff behind them all and the women at home trying to keep their dinners hot! As for the women whose men were in Caesar's or Alexander's or anyone else's army, all I can do is regret that so much of their story has been lost to humanity.

And so, gradually, it has dawned on me that a woman with a certain amount of education and leisure and space in which to reflect and to write her own story ought to do just that in order to help restore the balance. It is in this spirit that this account is offered – with its unresolved questions, frustrations and celebrations – memoirs from the margins of some important developments and happenings that have taken place during my lifetime and, with Kilroy, to say I was there. It is not intended, however, any more for women readers than for men. The hope is that it may be of some interest to both.

CHAPTER ONE

'But your beautiful life, James, your beautiful life ...'
– Nora Connolly, *Portrait of A Rebel Father*

The Spirit of God, the Holy Spirit, is, we are told, the Spirit of Truth. When other aspects of my faith seem at times to fall down around me I cling to this tremendous grab-hold; hold on to truth and you are holding on to God and before long 'the truth will set you free'. Of course in no time you will discover a certain sympathy with Pontius Pilate's plaintive (some say cynical) question: 'What is truth?' but surely his trouble was that he gave up the search rather too soon? Not that I haven't done likewise myself many times, but at least I seem to recognise when this has been so:

'Beauty is truth, truth beauty', said John Keats.
'That is all ye know on earth and all ye need to know'.
– 'Ode to a Grecian Urn'

Life is all about holding on to truth, holding on to beauty and not giving up on them.

As a child beauty for me was mainly to be found in my mother's lovely face, in the snuggling warmth of her cut-down squirrel coat, in the magic of the music and costumes for our annual dancing-displays in the Gaiety Theatre, in the perfume of the lilac tree in our front garden or of hyacinths in the house, in the flaming candles, the decks of flowers, the smiling Christ Child who beckoned me from the monstrance on a Holy Thursday altar, in the glory of stained glass, the rollicking of a polka, the pathos of a lullaby. Beauty could hit you anywhere – it still can. But I think I was more than a child when I first recognised beauty in the way so many 'ordinary' people handle their lives, coping cheerfully with the challenges facing them, radiating courage and kindliness around them often against the odds – a beauty which now for me reflects their Creator (whether they relate directly to Him or not) even more surely than does a heart-stopping symphony, a Western sunset or the incredible cadences of a willow-warbler.

'But your beautiful life, James? Your beautiful life?' James Connolly's wife, Lily, faltered when, on the eve of his execution, she visited him in Dublin Castle. This visit took place in the small room in which, not long ago, I was invited to meet the Taoiseach, Bertie Ahern, getting ready to host a huge Reception to mark the seventy-fifth anniversary of the Foundation of the State. Generosity, beauty, in that celebration? A Fianna Fáil Taoiseach acknowledging that the State was founded by the acceptance of the Treaty. Connolly's life had been beautiful, his wife considered, because he had tried hard to improve the lives of others. In what remains of my own privileged, sheltered one I would like to set out my stall of what I have known of beauty.

But I shall not be able to present this in a measured, orderly way. For one thing beauty is elusive, untameable, indefinable, isn't it? For another it often lies only in the eye of the beholder. Nevertheless I shall try to set down my story in a way which will share with its reader the goodness, the truth, the beauty I have known because, although these qualities are considered far from chic, and not attractive to many publishers, a great many hearts pine to hear more of them the world over.

There was a double finality about my father's death (10 July 1927). Not only was it the end of his own young life (he had just turned thirty-five years) but it was also the end of his dream of an early resolution of the partition of Ireland – a settlement to be reached through British and Irish acceptance of a system of Dual Monarchy. Moreover, ten years after his death a new Constitution was adopted, more confessional, more nationalistic than the one which he had piloted through the Dáil in 1922 and with it the Border became well and truly established, for better or for worse, not just territorially but also in the minds and hearts of people on either side of it.

Behavioural scientists recognise a certain syndrome that permeates some people upon the sudden death of somebody young and in the public eye. The assassination of President John F. Kennedy, the death of Princess Diana rocked millions around the world creating great waves of mourning and grief. In the 1920s, before the arrival of TV, the effect of the murder of the Vice President of the small Irish Free State, its Minister for Justice and for External Affairs was, of course, nothing as sensational, but nevertheless the killing of a young politician on his way to Sunday Mass in a quiet suburban area disturbed people very painfully and profoundly.

Many thousands queued for long hours to pass by his remains lying in state in the Oak Room of Dublin's Mansion House and the route of his funeral procession (which included twenty gun-carriages of wreaths) was packed with onlookers from Westland Row to Glasnevin Cemetery. It is only in recent times that I no longer meet people anxious to recall exactly where they were and what they were doing when they heard the news of his death. And many would tell of someone they knew who had been close to the scene, sitting on a nearby garden wall, soaring high on a swing, looking out an upstairs window, and so had been able to see the getaway car, even to take its number. As for the crowds of people said later that day to have called with messages of condolence to 'Dunamase', I would sometimes wonder if the Round Room in the Mansion House would have contained them all – let alone a private home. Perhaps one man encapsulated the whole phenomenon when he asked me with some astonishment whether in reality my father had been 'the man that died!' By then he had become almost a myth.

As I grew up and came to know more about his actual personality – mainly through his numerous very warm and human letters to my mother – I realised that the playful, ironic side of him might have enjoyed the joke, especially since it had centred on himself. Not that I think he would have wanted to belittle people's deep shock or sympathy or sense of loss, and I presume he would have been aware, also, how in such crises it can happen that some vulnerable people take the blame for the whole happening upon themselves, feeling the guilt of it as if they themselves had perpetrated it, but he could also have spotted the faintly ridiculous side of things and privately enjoyed it.

As a child I missed him dreadfully although I had no memory of him, being five months old when he died. But there seemed always to be this great hole, a vacuum filled with pain like the hollow that is left when a large tooth has been removed. The solemn, formal photographs in their black frames of the unsmiling 'late Mr. Kevin O'Higgins' with his outmoded stiff white collar, the boxes of yellowing newspaper clippings, were of little use to me. Privately I yearned for a father who would have been fun (something his letters conveyed), and who would have been proud of me like the father of my friend Ruth, or of my neighbour Norma. And always there was a sense of failure, of inadequacy – maybe especially so as his father too had been murdered and something bordering on Lady Bracknell's idea of carelessness would tend to infiltrate me. Other people had fathers, other people had grandfathers ... And so I would take myself away privately and weep – and weep.

Later it was the hangover from that aching and weeping that impelled me into helping to set up the Centre for Reconciliation at Glencree, County Wicklow, and into the peace movement of the seventies, eighties and nineties, because by then children on both sides of the political and sectarian divide in Ireland and children in our neighbouring island were likewise weeping and would be fathered only by photographs. This I felt I could not live with unless I could become involved in some alternative programme designed to improve the situation. And, of course, there was still the faint dream of a settlement with Northern Ireland, a dream that had died with my father in 1927, and again with the fall of the power-sharing Executive after Sunningdale, a dream of a settlement that people in both parts of the island and in Britain could live with.

Perhaps the dream of a Dual Monarchy (such as in Austria-Hungary and first worked upon in the Irish connection by Arthur Griffith) was never more than a dream, but it was one in which, for the final years of his life, my father strongly believed. Not long before his death he wrote fervently to my mother of 'going full steam ahead for a United Ireland' (an Ireland without a Border over which the British Monarch would reign as a kingdom separate and independent from Britain although sharing the same head of State). The Memorandum, placed before the British Cabinet by the Secretary for Dominion Affairs, L. S. Amery who, after discussions with my father, introduced these ideas to them, received an instant and frosty turndown, especially from the Foreign Secretary, Austen Chamberlain, and from Prime Minister Baldwin (Ref. DO 117/51 Public Records Office, Kew). Lord Carson by then retired, had not dismissed the idea when put to him informally by my father, whom Amery describes as being vibrantly an Irish patriot, and he continued to pursue the idea with zeal. He was, says the Dominions Secretary, possessed of an 'iron will' together with a 'gentle manner and great personal charm as well as a generous character and a broad outlook' and he was a man who continued to believe in his dream. 'His tragic death', continues Amery, 'was a dark stain on the troubled record of the Ireland of those years'. (L. S. Amery, *My Political Life*, Vol. 2. Hutchinson, 1953).

A Widow's Child

She kept a powder-puff of pale pink swansdown
placed in a bowl of coral-coloured glass
centred on her table;
candlesticks on either side,
made of the same pink crystal,
framed her pale face as she gazed
intently in her mirror.
Between them stood a cut-glass perfume-spray
with rubber bulb secured in silken netting
and a little dish of matching coloured glass
with upstretched finger to receive her rings.
Her sister made a frilly petticoat
to wrap around this marble table
hiding its naked timber uprights.
An ottoman stretched before the sun-filled window
covered in cheerful cretonne
and when it was cold, the gas-fire hissed a friendly singsong,
glowing in shades of pink and green and azure.

Within that room was focused all my being;
to it I turned for warmth, for comfort and for loving.
It took some time to understand the carved mahogany bed
was far too large for her small figure
and why the mirrored wardrobe, which was made for two,
held only female garments.
Three brass jugs that once warmed shaving-water
stood empty on the cupboard.
It took some time to realise
my mother too might need some comforting.

'... but we carried our brick and we laid it fair and square and as well as we knew how ...'

– Kevin O'Higgins

Considered in one way, the Good Friday Agreement of 1998 was not exceptionally long in coming given the depth of the mistrust and hatred that had preceded and indeed still surrounds it. But in the meantime how many precious lives have been wasted, shattered, oppressed? Each of us has only one life to live and to make beautiful. Before I die I should like to contribute something of beauty, if I can, as a small token of compensation for my privileged, sheltered upbringing.

Unfortunately, I have always had a talent for spotting a person's foibles rather too easily but I'm glad to say that I also feel very much alive to people's goodness and it is this that I most enjoy in life, believing, as I do, that it is God-with-us, a faithful presence in fulfilment of promises given.

Being faced with truth can, of course, be severely challenging at times. When I discovered that my young and over-stressed father had indeed become enamoured of the lovely Lady Lavery (and the letters as revealed for the first time by Sinéad McCoole in 1996 in her biography of *Hazel* are indisputable) truth seemed ugly, shocking. But since it was the truth then somehow, somewhere, there had to be beauty, freedom, in the revelation, in recognising and accepting it as truth. It was this freedom that gave me room for my public apology to the family of Lady Lavery (*Sunday Independent*, September 1996) and in 'This Week', on 'Radio Eireann' with Bryan Dobson. Previously, my father's biographer, Terence de Vere White, had been persuaded by some who had known her that Hazel Lavery had fabricated the story – an allegation which had deeply hurt her daughter Alice (Trudeau) Gwynn, who had written to him in protest and later in forgiveness, and for which I felt the need to express regret.

In his personal pursuit of truth and in fulfilment of his father's wishes, Roger Gannon, son of Bill Gannon (one of the three who had caused my father's death), sought me out some years ago to tell the story of the assassination as told to him, to his horror and amazement, by his father in his final illness (an account which has since been deposited by Roger in the National Archives ref. no. N.A.999/951). In Roger Gannon and, indeed, in his account of his father's character, is to be detected some of the sheer goodness of which I speak and which I see as God-with-us. That I can say this of people connected with the murder of my father and of a household which subscribed to no religion (Bill Gannon had been excommunicated in 1922 because of his membership of the IRA) may seem to some scandalous, but it has been my experience which I feel should be acknowledged. In their family the one binding precept was honour. Roger says if you gave your word it had to be honoured come what might. And he had given his word to his father he would tell the story.

Bill Gannon, while still a teenager, had been a member of Michael Collins' crack corps and had been involved with him in the murder of British plain-clothes detectives in their home on the morning of Dublin's Bloody Sunday in 1918. Collins was his hero but, unlike him, Gannon had subsequently taken the anti-Treaty side in the Civil War, some four years later taking part in the killing of Kevin O'Higgins, one of Collins' closest colleagues and greatest admirers.

It was only when Roger Gannon contacted me sixty years later that I learned that my father, with eight bullets in him, had actually managed to speak to his attackers on the roadside, telling them that he forgave them and that he understood why they had done it, but that this must be the last of the killings. Bill Gannon told his son that afterwards his whole life had been haunted by this happening. Although Collins had instructed his trainees never to leave a victim in agony but to finish him off, none of them could do it in this case. And so they went away leaving the still-conscious minister, his rosary beads in his hand, although they believed that he had recognised them and would soon identify them to the police.

But when my father was brought back to 'Dunamase', where he remained conscious for almost five more hours, speaking to family, colleagues and friends, nothing appears to have been said which would bear out that story, i.e. nothing was said about recognising anyone, speaking to anyone – only about forgiveness, about no bitterness

There are those who doubt if the encounter ever happened; they think instead that Bill Gannon either imagined or fabricated it. But from then on Gannon would only speak of O'Higgins as a 'very misunderstood man' and he would no longer carry a gun. Also something in his son's steely respect for the truth and his own reported unwillingness to 'shop around' for absolution from his excommunication, as many others did, causes me to think that Bill Gannon had not been given to playing with facts. But what the assassins did believe to have happened – *viz.* that my father had identified them *and* had given instructions that they were not to be pulled in (why else were they never stopped or challenged on their way to

Wexford they reasoned) – appears to me to have been unlikely. By all accounts that would have been untypical of his ideas of responsibility. I just believe that he died hoping, praying, that his would be the last of such deaths and that he kept silent about the encounter having no wish for three further deaths because of it.

You are invited to attend
a Memorial Mass for
KEVIN O'HIGGINS,
TIM COUGHLAN, ARCHIE DOYLE and BILL GANNON
which will be concelebrated
at the
Church of the Assumption, Booterstown
on Saturday July 11th at 11a.m.

My first meeting with Roger Gannon, in London not far from where he worked, was for me a traumatic undertaking. It was only when it dawned on me by degrees that, in fact, it was much more difficult for him to meet with me that I began to relax into what is now a very trusting relationship. He had first contacted me as a result of a notice which I had placed in newspapers in 1987, the 60th anniversary of the ambush, about a forthcoming Mass which would be offered by Father Enda McDonagh and many concelebrating priests for the souls of Tim Coughlan, Archie Doyle, Bill Gannon and Kevin O'Higgins (the first three having been named as the assassins for the first time in a recently published autobiography of Harry White, a well-known Republican, as told to Uinseann Mac Eoin). Another relation of Bill Gannon came to that Mass and was introduced to me by an *Irish Times* photographer who nobly refrained from taking our picture together. Things were not yet at that stage, not least because Special Branch minders of Garret FitzGerald, also present, were keeping an eye on him since he was a member of a Republican grouping. I found it moving that he had cycled a long way to get there and I invited him back to our house afterwards where he talked with Enda McDonagh, and also with one or two other people.

But Roger Gannon, when I eventually met him in London, was totally switched off from Republicanism, being very realistic about the relationship between Ireland and Britain where he was earning his living. Retired now from work, he still lives in England but retains vivid memories of his childhood in Dublin, stories which make excellent entertainment and which I hope someone will record. In spite of dyslexia, and without third level education, he has an impressive interest in art and in history, enhanced by frequent visits to London's galleries and museums. Having discussed the matter with his last remaining aunt and surrogate mother he went public with his testimony about my father's death, depositing his statement in the National Archives in Dublin (as I have mentioned) and broadcasting it in a programme on Radio Eireann presented by Myles Dungan and introduced by Professor Donal McCartney of UCD in which I also took part. 'Who are these people?' enquired a rather breathless photographer from the *RTÉ Guide* of my daughter Iseult, who was sitting in the outer studio. 'Oh', she said with some embarrassment, 'that man is just describing how his father murdered hers'. 'Really?' he said politely, getting his camera at the ready.

Something beautiful in this broadcast struck the then Archbishop of Dublin, Dr. Donald Caird, who told me afterwards that it was the most affecting piece of radio he had experienced. Maybe this was because, at a certain stage, Roger Gannon had become choked with tears, a son grieving, over sixty years later, for an act his father had committed before he was born. Roger is not at all convinced that there is a God, but his whole handling of this situation leaves me the more convinced that indeed there is.

Tim Coughlan was, I think, even younger than Bill Gannon when he took part in the murder of my father. Yet he died the following year, it is said in the home of a member of the Civic Guard.

I wonder how? I wonder why?

Archie Doyle, leader of the group and a builder in Rathgar, is well-documented in Harry White's book. Try as I may, I can find nothing beautiful in his reported triumphant dance on my father's grave but it was because of this that I had arranged the Mass for them all. In fact it was only because Enda at once responded to the idea of the Mass that I was able to stomach that piece of information and to get on with my life. Later, the fidelity of Roger Gannon in carrying out his father's wishes, and describing the effect my father's forgiveness had had on him, was the bonus from the God who has promised not to be outdone in generosity and who has, I trust, got all of them in his keeping.

Four years prior to the death of my father, his own father, a family doctor and coroner for County Laoighis, had been murdered in his home on a quiet Sunday evening, simply because he was the father of Kevin O'Higgins. This was in reprisal for the executions of four leading Republicans, among them Rory O'Connor, who had been a close friend of my father and his best man – 'the sublime Rory', as he refers to him in one letter written before the tragic parting of their ways. As it happened, my grandfather also had been a friend of O'Connor – a friendship formed when, at one stage, they had been jailed together and Grandfather had taken a professional interest in Rory's health. Now, two months after O'Connor's death, he was required to go further and to answer for that life with his own.

If there was beauty in this tragedy it had to be in my small grandmother's immediate insistence on forgiveness of it and upon no reprisals, in the courage of my teenage aunt, Patricia, who struck the gun out of the hand of one of the killers before cycling five dark February miles into Stradbally in search of a priest and a doctor. When considering forgiveness in Ireland I am drawn constantly back to my grandmother, who would give no evidence as to the identity of those involved although she almost certainly had recognised them. So nobody was ever charged. It was generally thought that they were neighbours, perhaps even patients of her husband, and she had had to lean across his prostrate body and hand them back the gun which he had managed to wrest from one of them before they would leave. Maybe, too, the night sky was beautiful, reddened as it was with the flames from the 'Woodlands' barns – the Higgins house had been raided thirteen times, mostly by Black and Tans, but more recently by Republicans.

Small and slight and gently spoken, Gran'ma nevertheless must have exerted considerable influence over her large family, however she achieved it. My father regarded her as a saint and, indeed, perhaps she was. How often I wished when my own family was young that I could produce a similar effect! There was a story that, when two of my uncles were disputing the ownership of a ball, one of them declared: 'It's mine because Mother says it is, and when Mother says it is, it IS – even when it isn't'. Later, these same sons would sit around her table, two on leave from British forces, others involved in Sinn Féin and on the run, and she would simply let it be known that politics were not to be discussed – so they were not.

The effect of his father's murder on my father was devastating – the more grievous because he himself was held to be the cause of it. But a few months later the Civil War was formally concluded and, on 7 June of the same year, his own birthday, his first child was born, Maev Brigid, to whom he looked as a symbol of hope, an olive branch, a new beginning.

FORGIVENESS

So there he stood upon the shore
with everything in waiting.
The fire was going well,
fresh fish were grilling
and they would bring some more
(this would confirm their own importance).
And at that Easter breakfast
he would hear from Peter
just how much he loved him
No decommissioning of the past
nor rank betrayals would be mentioned
simply 'Bring more fish' and 'Do you love me?'

Today as mists clear from the Agreement,
hammered in Belfast last Good Friday evening,
a voice speaks from far South Africa
of truth and reconciliation
and puts a definition on forgiveness:
'It is', the bishop says,
'a way of dealing with the past
so as to plan the future'.
Poor Peter's past had been disastrous
but he was asked to bring along his gifts
of fish and loving;
nothing more was needed
to complete this paschal sharing
and look towards the future.

CHAPTER THREE

'... and shelter me softly under the shadow of thy wings ...'
— Mrs Bessie Burgess in *The Plough and the Stars*

So there she was this new hope who, before long, became as firm and definite in her ideas as her father was in his. 'My Daddy rooned me!' she would complain when he gave her shining brown hair a pudding-bowl cut. 'My Daddy calls your little girl "Shove-on-and-push-her"' confidentially to the mother of Siobhán Leigh-Doyle. 'Holy little polar bear help me not to slobber' – praying aloud in Booterstown Church before the recumbent Lamb of God depicted above the high altar (being a city girl she was more familiar with animals in the Zoo, to which her father frequently brought her, than with lambs in the countryside, and on this particular Sunday he had been displeased with her table manners). 'Yes, but I didn't hear YOU tell Holy God you were sorry for slapping ME' to her maternal grandmother who had smacked her for rubbing sand in the eyes of her baby sister and who had said that, when they went to the church, she should tell Holy God she was sorry; Maev, who would later spend much of her life praying before the altar of God, but this time very privately. 'Won't you come and see us again?' the Mother Prioress of the Carmelite Convent in Blackrock asked her when, with her Nanny, she went there to collect the brown habit in which the remains of her father were to be laid out. Less than twenty years later she responded to that invitation, entering that enclosed community as a postulant and only moving from there in 1998 when it became necessary for it to disband, the individual members being received by other communities of the same Order.

Her birth had taken place from Government Buildings in 1923, where members of the Government and their families had had to live for several previous months under armed guard during the Civil War in order to keep the ship of State afloat. Some time – in the now fine Department of the Taoiseach, where the founding fathers with their wives once camped out in the old science labs, snatching a breath of air on the roof (only after darkness and never with a lighted cigarette in hand because of snipers from the roof of today's Merrion Hotel) some time it would be nice to have that part of the building's history remembered by a small plaque or an inscription. Bertie Ahern's generous and, one might even say, noble, words in Dublin Castle when marking the State's seventy-fifth birthday are, as I have said, among the beautiful things I have experienced and maybe they have brought the possibility of such a memento closer, a memento which would indicate that the founding fathers and mothers of the State had survived together for some time in that building, from which at least one child had been born.

At seventeen Maev's portrait was painted by the late Sean O'Sullivan R.H.A. 'She'll be a Reverend Mother', he confidently pronounced. And so she was, many years later, but not a high-profile *maitresse femme* which, perhaps, he had envisaged because when he knew her she was all go and full of projects. But the contemplative life which she chose, fearing that her interest in academic studies might distract her from God, has produced instead a more low-key woman, still very definite, still with a mind-blowing head for detail, but most anxious never to assert her own will, never to add to the burdens of others. Maev the leader, the 'head girl', the pathfinder, whose contemporaries at UCD – where she was awarded a First Class Honours Degree in Politics and Economics and won a Gold Medal for Legal Debate – remember her as always lively, involved in committees and with lots of friends, who later became a wise Prioress during difficult times for her Community – is still courageous and forward-thinking, but is anything but bossy.

In ways we are extraordinarily unlike. With powerful clarity of recall, Maev's memory can still be relied upon while whole swathes of detail have always passed me by without the slightest hope of being remembered. It can sometimes seem as if we are as mentally opposite as we were in appearance – she dark and rosy-cheeked, I a good deal taller, and fair, without any colour in my face. But if you want a sister who puts up with all your shortcomings and is never anything but utterly devoted to you, your spouse, your children and your grandchildren, and whose religious sisters are similarly inclined, then try to get yourself a Carmelite. Behind those grilles there are some wonderful women.

Being four years old when our father died, Maev knew him in a way I never did. A member of a large family, he seems to have been quite a 'hands-on' father who could be depended on for much 'walking the floor' with fractious infants and patient crooning of rhymes and verses to put children to sleep. Also he was a dab hand at bathing and feeding (I don't know about nappies). Strangely, although Maev can remember the great weeping at 'Dunamase' on the July Sunday of his death, what the cook said and did and how she went to the gate lodge to the gardener 'Mr. O' Bockie' and his wife for much of the day, she retains no conscious memory of her father himself. None at all. It is, perhaps, a classic case where a person blanks out something very painful.

An infant when he died, obviously I have no memory of him either. But in recent times, when so much more is known about the susceptibilities of infants and even of foetuses, and about the subconscious in general, and when so many people search for some memory of an unknown parent no matter how small, it has occurred to me to wonder about a slight pleasurable tingle in my left cheek at times. And I like to think this is my memory of a father who was in the habit of hoisting his babies on his shoulder, pressing his cheek to theirs to give comfort and support.

I would love to know what way our brother, born between Maev and myself, would have turned out. Finbarr Gerald, known as Barry, was born in November 1924, apparently a healthy, strong baby, but died two weeks later from pneumonia contracted, it was said, on the day of his baptism. For his mother, a widow's child with just one sister, the birth of a son was a total marvel; his death, after ten days of painful struggle, an agony. For his father (who sat up at nights with him in his distress) his death was so grievous he even, briefly, believed it to be the work of an enemy. But life would indeed have been difficult for a son of Kevin O'Higgins – my male cousins would have had had some taste of that – and Barry was taken before he really became part of his parents' lives. Or so one might think. My mother, on the other hand, would say that his loss was momentous for them both, something for her even to be compared with the subsequent loss of her husband. 'Dunamase' was decked with white flowers for his passing, and he is buried in Glasnevin cemetery in a grave where his father joined him less than three years later. Many years after that his mother, Brigid Cox, was also buried in that grave.

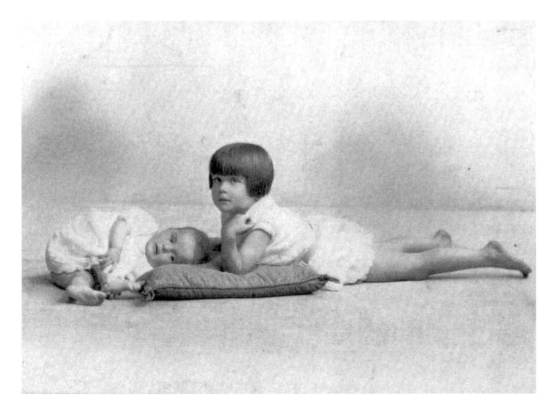

For my part I sometimes wonder whether Barry would have been the missing link between his sisters who are so different. Maybe he could have combined Maev's clarity of mind and grasp of facts with my sense of atmosphere and (rather sweeping) overview of things? If so, what a man he would have been!

JUST GOD

Details have always been a pain for me;
the names and years of wines, or species of plants,
or birds, or opus numbers of the music,
or recipes, or sporting teams
seldom remain –
only the fragrance, the taste, the flavour,
the marvellous 'birdness' of the creature,
the grace and courage of the players,
the sudden anguish of a cadence
or its mysterious assurance.

When someone speaks of God I like to hear,
God in the spare no-thingness of the deity, I mean,
not efforts to define, control, explain,
and not the news of the footsoldiers,
their holy networkings and tireless undertakings,
just God around, within, both them and me,
God in the quiet of a smile, a tear,
God in the freedom of abstractions,
in the silent grief of elephants over a dead companion
and in the buzzing of a sultry bee.

CHAPTER FOUR

'When Mother has a headache ... I'm as quiet as a mouse'

As I have said, the really beautiful thing for me in my childhood was my mother; the world centred around her, her smile meant everything. The glowing gas fire in her bedroom spelt out this message of warmth and love, its little flames of pink, blue, amber and green, toning with the rose-covered cretonne of her curtains, her bedspread and the ottoman in the south-facing bay window. And since she was so often laid low with prostrating attacks of migraine which lasted for days on end – brought on it was thought by the shock of her husband's death – quite a lot of my time was spent in that bedroom once the worst was over and she was able to communicate again. Her mother had come to live with us shortly after Daddy's death and Granny, often very worried by her daughter's state of health, would devote herself to nursing her. So I grew up in a household of women – my mother, my grandmother, and sometimes two indoor helps, with an extra woman who came on Mondays to wash and on Tuesdays to iron.

Always when something very important, like my First Holy Communion or a dancing display or a school play would be on the horizon, the big question would be whether Mother (we had umpteen pet names for her, but essentially she was 'Mother') would be well enough to be there. When she was, the whole scene would light up and I don't think it was so only for me. Most people seemed to find her charming. Hazel Lavery, on the other hand, considered her unutterably smug – or something like that. I find this a mystery because so many responded so favourably to her outgoing, friendly approach; indeed, she became a hard act to follow. ('Ah! You'll never be like your mother', would reach my ears so often when I was growing up). Maybe it was that Hazel, realising the way her friendship with my father was shaping, wanted to blame my mother for not stepping in and resisting it. But my mother didn't do that because, while she certainly knew her husband greatly admired Lady Lavery and valued the assistance she was giving to the emerging State, she probably never understood the depth of that admiration.

After the sale of 'Dunamase' a few months after the death of my father, the house to which we moved was in Cowper Gardens, near to Beechwood Avenue Church. This house was called 'Knockbeg' after the college in County Carlow where my parents had met when my mother was on the teaching staff, and my father, Sinn Féin T.D. for the area and on the run, had been given refuge from time to time.

My mother's maiden name was Cole; her first name was Brigid, or 'Birdie'. Her academic career had been distinguished – prizes, medals and 'exhibitions' (as scholarships were then called) all the way, ending up with First Place and First Class Honours in her Degree (with English as her major subject). Knockbeg College was then a minor seminary and the bishop of that diocese had asked that the top graduate of that year be offered a position there so as to improve the schools results in English examinations. When this turned out to be a woman, credit must be given to all concerned that they held to their course. There was no other female on the teaching staff – let alone a young and pretty one. It must have been lonely for that solitary woman at times in that old and rather draughty building with the mists from the River Barrow pervading a winter's day, but she always spoke of the boys, the priests, and the other 'professors' with enthusiasm. She had not wanted to leave Dublin where she had a large circle of friends (male admirers had struck up 'Oh, you beautiful doll!' from the back of the hall when she was being awarded her degree), but a job was a job and this was a good one. Long years afterwards at the wedding of our eldest son, Kevin, to Annemarie Linehan, the bride's grandmother told me that she had known about my mother's being in Knockbeg because she herself, at the same time, was also teaching in a seminary and that they were then the only two women in Ireland so engaged.

Much of the courtship of my parents had to be conducted through letters. The postal service seems to have been magnificent. If a letter posted in Dublin did not reach County Carlow the following day, there would be considerable anxiety; were the letters of this man on the run being intercepted? I have found it a blessing indeed that he committed so much to paper. Mother kept all his letters but destroyed her own (which he had retained) after his death. Reading his for the first time as I did when I was young and romantically-minded, I found them refreshing and invigorating – straightforward, humble, brave, humorous. Others will understand better the political background from which he was writing, but for me they contained the essential thing – a real person to whom one could relate, a sporting, unselfish character as good as any 'Scarlet Pimpernel' or other hero one might read about.

Such was the power of love, nothing seemed a problem to him. Gloomy digs were the homes from which, under various pseudonyms, he would cycle to Dalkey, Rathfarnham or Dundrum to visit various relatives and take his 'kid sisters' out of boarding school for a treat. Tickets for the current shows would be bought for them and for my mother's sister (Mollie – our Aunt Mo) and he would keep regular touch also with his aunts in Marlborough Road. At the same time he would be sending these almost daily missives to his sweetheart as well as cigarettes (which he believed necessary for her nerves), magazines and gallons of a tonic which seemed good just then, and whatever else she asked for. The letters, of course, are full of references to the politics of the time – to raids on the offices in which he was working, for instance, but such things are reported in a breezy, light-hearted way so as not unduly to arouse her fears. He tells how frustrated he is by the curfew, about his certainty that Sinn Féin will win through before long – matters better left to a historian to relate. For me there remains indelibly the background picture of a generous-hearted, affectionate, courageous man, coping lightly with such things as painful dental and ear abscesses, giving up smoking and going vegetarian, while pouring out his devotion to his girl and all the time doing his best to 'save the nation' (as I might call it).

As to how he subsequently became enthralled by Hazel Lavery I have no knowledge, but of one thing I have always been certain – he was far from the cold-hearted figure of popular myth. One is left guessing what emotional price was paid for being central to such tragedies as the execution of his best man, Rory O'Connor, the murder of his father, and the burning of his first marital home, and one can only conjecture what forces beset him after the price was paid.

On Reading the Letters of my Father to Hazel Lavery

— Easter 1995

'Come take my hand' you say 'and walk upon the waters'.
'The waters of betrayal, Lord? Uncompassed and afraid,
bereft without my certainty, my Dunamase, my citadel,
bronze figure of antiquity in Churchill's ringing phrase?'

'But take my hand' you coax 'and tread upon the waters'.
'Deep waters of depression, dejection or despair?
grey waters of bewilderment, of cynical surrender,
or shallows of distraction over which to sail elsewhere?'

'Come take my hand' you plead 'and test my shining waters'
come walk on sparkling waters in the radiance of the sun;
bright waters of complexity, humanity, diversity,
clear waters of forgiveness, of compassion and of love.

For absolutes belong to me and no-one else is sacred
and bronze can be the stuff of which false images are formed;
and people are not images but flesh and blood and fragile,
come, celebrate the doting 'hands-on' Father of them all!

But the 'Knockbeg' that I knew, the house in which I spent my childhood, contained only such things as his *Dáil Reports*, his copy of *The Big Fellow* (Piaras Beasley's life of Michael Collins), the brass jugs which had kept warm the water for his shaving. Those were the days in which there was always a 'good room' or two in middle class houses – rooms which were only used on Sundays or on special occasions. In 'Knockbeg' the diningroom was such a room with its large mahogany table and dining chairs with rawhide seats (I loved surreptitiously peeling little bits off them, though of course I wasn't meant to). There was a Dun Emer rug on the floor and the curtains were of the same shade of smoky blue with Celtic hand-done embroidery at the hem. All these had come from 'Dunamase', together with the bow-fronted Sheraton sideboard (something I still retain) on which Mass had been celebrated after my father's death. On the walls were some prints from the Cuala Press:

We are less children of this clime
than of some nation yet unborn
or empire in the womb of time.

(Is A.E.'s empire nearer now after the Good Friday Agreement of '98?);

Pedlar of dreams when our toil is ended and days grow old
and rooks fly homeward on dark wings bended
through dusky gold ...

God keep my jewel this day from danger
from tinker and pookah and blackhearted stranger ...

These too had come from 'Dunamase' where there had been many dinner parties so that each District Justice, Circuit Court, High Court and Supreme Court judge and other such dignitaries could get to know the Minister for Justice in his own home. But the portrait of my mother, painted by Sarah Purser not long after my father's death, was never on display in Knockbeg because the sitter disliked it and so it had to be content to hang behind a curtain in a sort of dumping area known as 'the black hole'. Nevertheless, I like to hang it now, although facially it is not very like her, since the aura of it conjures up something of her for me as she was in those days.

The diningroom was used for parties, an occasional lunch or supper for friends of my mother, card parties once or twice a year for my grandmother's friends (mostly Brutons, related to the former Fine Gael leader), and parties for us children which, of course had to include children you hardly knew but whose parents had entertained your mother. For these occasions an extra leaf had to be inserted into the dining table and I remember a ghastly moment when I saw it tilting towards the daughter of the Polish Minister and depositing jellies and meringues into her lap. For such festivities we wore organdie, velvet or taffeta dresses with 'puff' sleeves (organdie scratched your arms!) and beforehand the ends of our lamentably straight hair would be turned up with curling tongs. Sometimes when passing a hairdressing salon nowadays I get that slight singeing smell wafting out to the street and I am back for a moment to the days of parties, dancing displays and other big moments of my early childhood.

Of course, like most children, my life at that time was about learning things – or trying to learn them. Sums to me would always remain a mystery, although Maev spared no pains in trying to teach me all she knew. Three-and-a-half years older, she was brave and clear-headed and loved to produce her little sister so that she even managed to get me on to the stage of the Gaiety Theatre at the age of two-and-a-half in order to 'say my recitation'. That poem was indeed appropriate –'When Mother has a headache / I'm as quiet as a mouse ...' since, as I have said, our poor mother was afflicted for many years with the most devastating and frequent attacks of migraine, brought on by shock. But back to the Gaiety stage and to the Annual Dancing Display put on by Miss Muriel Catt, and Maev's persuading Miss Catt that I should join in! Absolutely terrified I got through my party-piece somehow by saying it up to 'Daddy Tim' seated in what is known nowadays as the Presidential box. I can still see the white-bearded face of the Governor-General, my father's uncle, T. M. Healy (whose granddaughters attended the same dancing school), bending down kindly to catch what I was saying. It is hardly likely that anyone else heard a thing!

Not too long after making my début in this way, I joined 'Miss Catt's' myself and became enthralled by the excitement of these annual Displays. Probably the most memorable thing was having the full Gaiety orchestra under the baton of 'Uncle Nobby' (Raymond Nobarro) accompanying us. We sprang as grasshoppers, hovered as clouds, flew as birds, bees and butterflies, swirled as gypsies and floated(?) as fairies and ballerinas to the most lovely music only heard, prior to that, on Miss Catt's upright piano.

I played 'The Pied Piper of Hamelin' when I was a bit older and, to my horror, nearly lost some of the tiny children dancing aroundme because they let go hands when in a fast-moving 'buzz', and would have tumbled down on top of the orchestra if Miss Catt and her assistant had not dashed out from the wings and gathered up armfuls of them. As 'Snow White', a real boy playing the prince had to waken me with a kiss and in the confusion I managed to part from my long black wig. As Ellie in 'The Waterbabies', the white swimsuit which I wore offended the elderly lady next door when she saw me subsequently sporting it in our back garden: 'Put some clothes on that child!'

Once Maev and I had a duet as 'Happy Hikers' (mainly Maev starred in 'speaking parts' because she had a prodigious memory and could generally be relied on to keep the whole show on the road) in which, after sixteen bars of introduction we were supposed to abandon our picnic lunch and get up to dance. However, on the day, there were real sandwiches and lemonade for the lunch instead of pretend ones and, thirty-two bars later I thought 'Uncle Nobby' was looking a bit feverish. But still there was no way I was going to get to my feet unless Maev went first – she was always in charge.

The costumes for these displays were thrilling and I loved the whole colour and magic of them. But of course there were many ordinary, sometimes dreary afternoons as well, of routine classes and rehearsals which meant toting satchels and dancing-things to 120 Lower Baggot Street after school, where it wasn't always warm and where Miss Catt might not be in her best mood.

Grown-ups sometimes held parties for children also, even when they had no children of their own. The Consul General for the Netherlands used to host a party for young people at the hotel in Harcourt Street, where he lived. At such an occasion there would be a cinematograph show – in his case there would be films about the Dutch Queen Wilhelmina and her daughter Princess Juliana. I'm not sure that I was totally comfortable at such gatherings but he was very kind and the food was lovely so that I got over his referring to us as 'yungsters' and just put it down to his being foreign. Another moment that took getting used to was when one little girl would appear in a long dress with pearls in her hair and could curtsey to my mother or to whoever was hosting the party. Her mother also was foreign so you couldn't pass any remarks about her quaint ways.

The drawing-room in 'Knockbeg' was another 'good room'. Northward facing, it was not very inviting except in wintertime with a good fire. Unfortunately, the piano was kept there and, searching for excuses as to why I did not make better progress with that instrument, I blame the fact that one bar of an electric heater doesn't do much to take the chill off a not-much-lived-in fairly large space. The piano itself was pretty, however, with its brass candlesticks and orange silk vest, but it was a bit lonely having to go there and 'do my practice' and, consequently, I was not very diligent about it. Now if the piano had been in the family room or in the diningroom – both south-facing ...?

Upstairs on the bedroom level there was a large landing where we could practise difficult bits in a dance routine or complicated exercises with skipping ropes (because Miss Catt taught dancing AND callisthenics, something, I think, to do with skipping ropes and barbells and Indian clubs).

Marvellous parties for children were held also at 'Shamrock Hill', nowadays Donnybrook Castle, and 'Glenaulin', the homes of Healy and Sullivan cousins and grandaunts. Although both houses were inhabited only by adults, children were allowed to run free in them, to have treasure hunts and to play hide-and-seek all over the place, never mind the collections of Waterford glass, jade, antique snuff boxes and the like. And each child would always get a prize, a really good one. These were houses to which we were frequently invited, even when there wasn't an actual party on. Sunday afternoons were the time for the clan to gather – to swim or go boating in the lovely foaming Liffey which bordered the garden of Glenaulin, to play croquet or sit under the willow tree at Shamrock Hill listening to jokes and funny stories before tucking in to sumptuous teas. 'My pet, you've eaten nothing!' Auntie Maev Sullivan would mourn, although by then you were so full you could hardly utter; Auntie Maev, the gentlest spoken lady I ever knew and probably the most determined. To us and, even more so, to her Healy nieces and nephews, she was a sort of fairy godmother who would meet you in Grafton Street on your birthday and urge you to choose in Brown Thomas' whatever gift you wanted! The children of her friends and neighbours similarly remember her bounty. As a girl she had studied painting in Paris; a still-life of hers which she gave us as a wedding present remains as a treasured memento of her, admired by our friends.

Her sister, Lizzie Healy in 'Glenaulin', whom we called Auntie Ea, had been hostess for her father, Tim Healy, at the Vice Regal Lodge when he was Governor-General, her mother having become an invalid. Lizzie, again at her best with children, was shy with adults and her short-sightedness caused her to screw up her face when she was addressing you, something which caused guests at the Vice Regal at times to consider her haughty. But we always found her fun, ready to bob up and down in the river with you, her white curls peeping out from under her bathing cap and somehow never getting wet.

Uncle (granduncle) Tim Sullivan at Shamrock Hill was one of my pin-up people, always ready with a smile or a funny song, or parodies which he would compose on well-known numbers. His brother, Chris, who lived in Anglesea Road with three of their sisters (still known as 'the girls') was a positive hero, because 'the Anglesea Roads' sometimes took a house in Sandycove at the same time as we went there on holidays and Uncle Chris would devote himself to watching and encouraging our swimming lessons (with a Captain Gillespie, on the end of a long pole with a canvas belt around your middle). Uncle Chris, retired from the Royal Navy and whose Bantry background further linked him to the sea, would try also to explain to us how ships kept upright in the water and how sailing boats sailed. Digging deep into his not over-stocked pocket he even bought us each a model sailing boat with perfect rigging (but, child-like, I still privately preferred the crude little red and white job I had bought with half-a-crown of my own money in Woolworth's in Dun Laoghaire). On a marvellous day at Bullock Harbour he rescued a tiny kitten from drowning, pumping out its tiny lungs with his doctor's hands. 'Moses', as he became known, then went on to become a stately and prosperous cat back in Anglesea Road. Uncle Chris could tell you about the first motion picture he saw; after queuing for a long time he went in to see a wave breaking on a rock for a few minutes and then to see, though not hear, a lion roaring. It had been a wonderful show! I adored the way he would call me 'Billie' and would promise me a shilling if I could keep up my prodigious nosebleeds for another five minutes – somehow I never could. He would tap out tunes on his glass eye too; he was the only true 'súil amháin' of the clan, he said.

'The girls' – grandaunts Katie, Fanny and Josephine – were similarly interested in children. Visits to them could be hilarious although all we did was sit around and tell stories and have tea (not quite on the scale of 'Shamrock Hill'). Fanny, with her melting brown eyes, had been my father's godmother, often referred to in his letters, and he had visited them a good deal when they lived in Marlborough Road. Much of their time was spent in Donnybrook Church just across the road from them in Anglesea Road – the church to which their sister, Annie, my grandmother, made her way to 7.30 am Mass on foot, winter and summer, day in and day out. After the death of her husband she had moved to Dublin to be near all these relations and lived at No. 99 Marlborough Road.

'You could set your clock by her', some of the neighbours said, referring to her tripping past their doors each morning on her way to Mass.

By the time I knew them, these clan elders seemed to be apolitical. Probably the effect of the Parnell split had left the families of Tim Healy and of T. D., A. M. and D. B. Sullivan with little enthusiasm for further altercations. Earlier, at least some of 'the girls' had been active in the Gaelic League; Aunt Fanny favoured mostly Irish tweeds and woollens in her modest wardrobe and Aunt Jo always wore her Tara brooch (together with dark-ribbed stockings and high button boots) no matter what. Their father, T. D. Sullivan, had been an MP, had edited *The Nation* newspaper, had founded *The Irish Catholic* and had composed many ballads including the stirring 'God Save Ireland'. While Lord Mayor of Dublin he had been imprisoned in Maryboro Jail. During Tim Healy's period as Governor-General they visited the Vice-Regal Lodge (now Áras an Uachtaráin) almost every Sunday – as did my father and mother frequently. These visits must have required some nifty footwork at least on the part of the ladies, since protocol then required that you never turned your back on His Excellency and, if leaving a room before he did, you had to back out curtseying three times as you went! My father privately felt that if he were in politics at the time of the Parnell controversy, he would have sided with 'the Chief', but he wasn't, and I expect he kept these sentiments to himself in clan circles in which, initially at least, he was a country cousin from a junior branch. After his death, which took place in the same week as that of his aunt, the wife of Tim Healy, my mother and I spent several weeks in the Vice-Regal Lodge, and 'Daddy Tim', as I grew to call him, was a sort of Santa Claus figure in my early childhood, sometimes appearing at 'Knockbeg' in a large car with a bag of his peaches and pears (of which he was very proud). I don't read today's scathing biographies of him; I think only of the spirited *No Man's Man* written by his daughter, Maev. In that no doubt I am biased, lacking in openness, but I want to hold on to that kind face bending over the box in the Gaiety and willing me through my piece – in spite of my terror.

'Aunt Haddie' (widow of D. B. Sullivan), who lived in Greystones and whom we used to visit quite a lot, having picnics and bathing parties from her house 'Dunboy', had become friendly with Sinéad Bean de Valera when they were both enthusiastic members of the Gaelic League before the Split. After the Treaty was signed Mrs. de Valera told Aunt Haddie how sorry she was that now they could no longer be friends, but that she would always retain in her heart the kindness Aunt Haddie had shown to herself and to her children when her husband had been away in America and times had been hard for them. At that time too Michael Collins used to make regular trips to Greystones to check on the welfare of Dev's family and it was in Greystones, while staying with the Sullivans, that my mother spent one terrible night during which she kept imagining that Bray Head was all on fire and that the whole map of Ireland was burning. The next day she learned of the death of Michael Collins.

There were divided opinions in the clan as to what should be done about one of its members, Maimie Gavan Duffy, daughter of A. M. Sullivan, whose husband had signed the Treaty but had later voted against it. My grandmother held that this should make no difference at all to her friendship with her cousin, but one of my aunts thought otherwise. The story was that this aunt had had to dive for cover under the dining table when Gran'ma deliberately invited Maimie to stay to tea, and there was no other escape. Fortunately, it was a large table with one of those heavy cloths with bobbles under the white tea-cloth, so all that was needed was patience.

If in my childhood beauty for me lay more in the elegant houses and lovely gardens of Shamrock Hill and Glenaulin, which were tended with such constant care by Auntie Maev, Auntie Ea and Joe Healy's wife, Auntie May (always with a twinkle in her eye and game for a laugh), with hindsight I tend to think more of the beauty in the concern of those relatives for us and the support which it meant to our mother. When, in time, I was expecting my own first child I turned at once to Dr. Tim Healy (son of 'Daddy Tim') in whom I had always had enormous trust, especially since the time when, as a child, he had taken me in Glenaulin's wooden canoe (a gift from native

Americans to Ireland's Governor-General) and had gone a little too close to the weir. Crazily we spun around for a few moments but he managed to bring us safely home. And I felt sure he would do the same for my children.

CHAPTER FIVE

'Where are we now?'

But of course life wasn't all about parties and holidays, more about lessons, which I mostly enjoyed (except for anything to do with sums), and about music exams or Feiseanna – I went to Belfast to compete in the under-nine class – and about dancing exams also. Our Preparatory School, St. Anthony's in Hatch Street, was run by Miss Beales who before long became Mrs. Nicell. There we learned Irish and French from an early age. Although always scared of mice, I felt warm towards 'Madame Souris' and her family who lived in a house made of 'fromage'. We sang hymns and had May processions and went from there to the Convent of Marie Reparatrice in Merrion Square to be prepared for our First Holy Communion by Mother St. Barbara in her wonderful habit of cream and aquamarine. I was five and by then had got this thing about forgiveness firmly in my mind; you couldn't receive Jesus and tell Him you loved Him unless you forgave everybody, even those who had murdered your Daddy. I don't remember discussing this with anybody – it was just something that seemed to follow naturally from what was being said about loving God and when, at times, I am tempted to wonder whether there is a God at all, it is my mainstay. Someone put into me that conviction about the necessity of forgiveness, Someone gave it to me as a gift and, as far as I am concerned, that Someone is God.

From St. Anthony's I went, at the age of eight, to the Convent of the Sacred Heart in Lower Leeson Street for the next eight years of schooling. By the time I arrived there, Maev was blazing a trail which became a hard act to follow. In fact, I'm not sure that I tried all that hard to follow it, what with the sidelines of piano lessons and dancing lessons and, in the summer terms, being plagued with hay fever. But I came alive for the school plays, although they had their hazards; as Jephthah's dead daughter, being wafted by angels through the skies on a make-shift tray seemed all too realistic! And I loved the choir and the poetry of the little Office of the Immaculate Conception – 'O Lady make speed to befriend me/ From the hands of the enemy mightily defend me/ Hail Gideon's fleece, Hail blossoming rod/ Sampson's sweet honeycomb, Portal of God' – and the serenity of the chapel with its beautiful stained glass windows.

Being Maev's sister meant, of course, trying in turn for one's pink, green and blue ribbons – distinctions awarded 'by the votes of the pupils ratified by the religious' – and eventually I did manage to achieve these, although with some difficulty. Growing into my teens was a lot more problematical than had been my earlier development. I don't think that this had as much to do with my mother's second marriage (although that certainly presented challenges for all concerned) as it had to do with my own introspective insecurity. I remember being excessively sensitive about whether or not my friends *were* my friends, about growing much taller than Maev, about having to wear some of my mother's cast-off clothes (bought in Marjorie Boland's or even Miss Doran's, no less, but much too grown-up for me, I reckoned).

There was, however, at least one outfit of my mother's which I was glad to inherit, a pretty, brownish-pink tweed 'costume', i.e. jacket and skirt, the former belted with big patch pockets and the skirt box-pleated. This was a number from Miss Doran's but of course I removed the label in case my friends might see it. A popular indoor item in a female wardrobe at that time would be a 'twin-set' (matching jersey and cardigan), worn often with 'Gor-Ray' skirts. For weddings or the Horse Show, or such like, women might wear an edge-to-edge lightweight coat over a floral silk dress with a hat or beret made of the same material as the coat, and for anything at all formal gloves and hats would be worn by daughters and mothers alike. In Dawson Street, as well as Miss Doran, 'Madame Foin' had an establishment where she structured 'foundation garments' to support the particular contours of each client, while in Grafton Street, 'Marjorie Boland's' and in Wicklow Street 'Mansfield Sisters' held delights for brides, for debutantes and for 'the older woman'.

My mother paid for major items in my wardrobe such as my 'coming out' dress from Marjorie Boland's (white chiffon, edged with silver bugle beads) but I had an allowance out of which I paid for the rest of my finery, and I remember splurging £5 on a fur coat in Clery's, which never really recovered from the first shower of rain it encountered. Since there were still porters to be had, vast amounts of luggage were usually brought when travelling, with special cases for hats and shoes. My aunt's cat, unfortunately, took a fancy to my Confirmation hat in its box in the bottom of the wardrobe and decided to have her kittens in it. This was when I was staying with her on a holiday, very proud of my new coat with its matching sailor hat. Until then the cat had been known as 'William', but promptly was renamed 'Gladys' by my uncle. Something apparently almost totally disappeared from today's stores, but so appreciated then, are chairs for the weary shopper. At that time you might know by name the attendant behind the counter and she would take out drawers full of stockings, gloves, lingerie, handkerchiefs, or whatever else you might be in search of, while you could often take home two or three garments 'on appro' to be decided on at a later stage.

But I have gone too far ahead and am still only a schoolgirl.

On the plus side I became keen on tennis, at which I proved to be a lot better than hockey, and at the age of thirteen I lost my heart to the Captain of Clongowes, the first of many such casualties!

What remains for me of Leeson Street are the extraordinarily varied personalities of some of the nuns: the flair and verve of the American Mother Lombard; the gentleness and delightful good humour of Mother Kerr (an aunt of the Duke of Norfolk); the drive and teaching skill of Mother Hogan; the patience and prayerfulness of the Sister from Alsace who sat at the door and always smiled but spoke little English. Annual plays produced by Mother Sheehan or by Mother Rita O'Donoghue were important occasions into which a lot of effort was put. Emphasis was placed also on the singing of Plain Chant and our choir made some broadcasts from Radio Eireann in Henry Street, something I found exciting. Games and drill were coached by Miss Meldon, to stirring Souza marches. Music lessons by then for me were at the Read School of Music in Harcourt Street, lessons for which I never seemed to have done sufficient practice but which I enjoyed, always believing that I really *would* work harder next week. In school most subjects were not a problem, except that maths still remained a mystery, and I seemed to spend much of geography classes checking the rainfall in a small receptacle placed on the back lawn. At 'recreation' we played a team game which we called baseball and which, I think, was an upgraded form of rounders. It worked well because I don't remember people standing about feeling left out of things. Friends I made at that time of my life are still my friends. At Leeson Street Maev shone, carrying off endless prizes and ribbons and generally blazing a trail which, as I have said, would have been impossible to live up to. I think I decided I wouldn't attempt the impossible and continued to mosey on fairly comfortably. Until I went to Mount Anville!

In 1940 when Mother married the well-known solicitor, Arthur Cox, I was thirteen and Maev had turned seventeen. Home then became 'Carraig Breac' a beautiful house at the Baily surrounded by seventeen acres of woodland, heather and gardens – truly a fairyland with all the wonders and, for me anyway, some of the loneliness of the same. The formal gardens, lovingly created by the Stokes family (the Japanese garden of miniature bonzai trees and shrubs particularly fascinated me) – the marvellous rhododendron and azalea walks and perhaps, especially, the wild heather and gorse leading up to the 'Carraig' at the top, were enchanting. From the 'Carraig' you could see the whole of Dublin Bay and make it your own. On a clear day you could see the Welsh coast – but that was a sign of bad weather coming.

It was in Carraig Breac that I spent my teens and I think I developed there a sense of apartness, of aloneness that has had advantages and disadvantages for me in later life:

There is an azalea with a certain flower
of shocking orange sherbet
which with its special fragrance
can suddenly transport me to a hillside bower
of near-forgotten girlhood's hopes and dreams
its unrealities – its devastating loneliness

At first my major preoccupation was in sort of excusing Carraig Breac, explaining it away to my school friends so they wouldn't envy me too much and spoil our relationships. Can too much beauty do this to people? At that stage I certainly feared it might. But at the same time the very beauty itself, the fearlessness of the Carraig, the haunting fragrance of the flame and yellow azaleas, the wise shelter of the choice rhododendrons brought back by Lady Stokes from her travels in India and China, the green mystery of the 'Maryland' woods, the cheerful bravery of the daffodils and snowdrops under overhanging trees took over much of my spirit and strengthened it.

The house was old and not very large, full of character with diamond-paned windows and a graceful semi-circular staircase. With hindsight I regret that it was furnished mostly with Millar and Beatty reproduction furniture, except for the drawing room suite of Chinese Chippendale, but I realise that these were the war years and also that there would have been practical reasons why this was so.

Teens are notoriously a difficult time and mine began with an almost complete make-over, e.g. from never having had a family car I was now riding in a chauffeur-driven Dodge, from linoleum in all but the 'good rooms', there was now wall-to-wall carpeting everywhere. It says a lot for my mother and all concerned that I did not become more volatile than I did. If at first I found it hard to get accustomed to our new step-father with his sometimes embarrassing idiosyncrasies, I grew before long to develop an almost unspoken rapport with him and to appreciate his goodness. We shared a devotion to dogs – he being, however, more lenient towards their misbehaviour, more egalitarian in outlook about their 'rights' and dignity in their own home. 'Does Jack [John A.] Costello ever bring Slemish [his dachshund] to Court?' my mother once asked, desperate to draw Arthur into a conversation with guests from whom so far he had been rather withdrawn. 'Only for really important cases', he replied, with one of his famous grins.

That was largely his way at home – a world of as much make-believe as possible, of pipe-smoking, of detective stories, of walks through the woods with a mischievous dog ecstatically pulling out of his untied shoe laces, while Percy, the cat, might drop down with insouciance from an overhead branch, just happening to be going the same way. It was a world to which I found it easy to relate. When I was in boarding school he would write about it to me – long hand-written letters about made-up people based on the characters of our dogs. His professional life was enormously stressful at the time, since he had set up most of the new semi-State companies and many others. But he could switch off completely when he came home, late though it was, and did not make a practice of taking work home with him.

It was 'the Hare' Guinness, who lived at 'Danesfort', the neighbouring property, who had encouraged Uncle Arthur to buy 'Carraig Breac'; they were friends and business associates. Another neighbour was Harold Maxwell of Maxwell Weldon's (solicitors) so Arthur came complete with a passport into the rather exclusive society of 'the Hill'. Nowadays, the names Howth, Sutton and the Baily are often interchangeable – NOT THEN. The Hill was the Hill was the Hill. The emphasis was on gardens, on humanitarian good works, on a certain frugality. Arthur's asceticism delighted his neighbours. Before long he had garaged the Dodge and returned his petrol ration to the Government in case it were needed for more important work. Not quite a vegetarian (he sometimes ate a tiny lamb cutlet), his diet was meagre and he was a teetotaller.

Meantime my mother, and a marvellous cook, Mrs Fuller, whose sister worked next-door in Guinness's, struggled to keep things as normal as possible in spite of shortages due to the war. I remember experiments with cooking in a hay box, large crocks of water-glassed eggs and coffee made with dandelion roots. Michael Doyle, who assisted Mr. Moody in the garden, managed to keep SOME heat in the central heating furnace in the winter months, and all went well in 'Carraig Breac'. That is, it went well for us. Not for much of the rest of the world, as would become clear when we turned on the 'wireless' in the evening to listen to the news.

Teenage years are highly impressionable ones, as most people know. Mine were certainly deeply affected by reports of the war, in particular by thoughts of bombings of civilian populations. As a child I had spent many very happy holidays with Auntie Mo and Uncle Harry Schofield, Mother's beloved sister and her husband (whom I adored), who lived in Lancashire and who had brought us on visits also to Edinburgh and to London. 'Doctor', as this uncle was known to one and all – it was his pet name – was in general practice outside Manchester and we would go driving with him quite a lot, so that I felt I knew people who would be undergoing those air raids. In the early mornings while it was still dark I had heard the clip-clop of the Lancashire clogs on the cobbled streets when miners and mill workers were making their way to work. Now they were making munitions instead, and where was beauty to be found in the fact that so many would be killed? The Irish have never been admiring of Winston Churchill, but I still think we owe a tremendous debt to him for being what he was during those terrible years. From the point of view of Anne Frank (approximately my own age but *so* much more mature) and others like her, there was a tremendous problem to be experienced, a problem in which it was only possible to think of God as a suffering God, suffering with his people in the concentration camps and in the gas chambers, and in the bombardment of cities like Coventry, Birmingham, Dresden and Cologne. But that God, while his beauty was certainly hidden, still maintained his Truth in the testimony of Dietrich Bonhoeffer and Maximilian Kolbe and no doubt of many others about whom we have never heard.

At the Baily the war was particularly anxious, not because the word EIRE was painted in very large white letters on the Baily Green, but because anybody who was anybody had a son or daughter or other relative engaged in it. (At Carraig Breac we were all too conscious that Mrs. Fuller's husband was serving with a tank corps). 'Where are we now?' called from one end of the Hill tram from an enquirer, who had got on before the news of that day had been broadcast, to another traveller who had boarded further down the Hill and who would have had more time to hear it, meant, of course, not 'At what stage of our journey are we?', but 'How are Our Boys doing today?'

The new State into which I had been born was only twenty years a-growing. Many of the neighbours had served in British forces at an earlier time (you could mostly tell it by the high polish on their leather shoes) and this was war. At the same time they prized their Irishness and made efforts to belong in Ireland – as they understood it. I remember meeting Miss Guinness, from Ceanchor, going off to have lunch with Mr. de VALera (as she pronounced it) in high delight and draped in a voluminous cape of Irish tweed and matching beret with Tara brooch well to the fore. Further up the Hill, Lady Yarrow, at 'Journey's End', in an effort to learn Irish would, although very elderly, cycle down to Sutton, putting her bike on the tram for the return journey. Recently she had become a Catholic – mostly because of St. Francis of Assisi and his love of animals. Antivivisection was her big cause and I met her one morning climbing into the tram in a long black velvet gown and what was obviously her best hat (although somewhat antique) on her way to be Confirmed at the Franciscan Church on Merchant's Quay. The tram was a wonderful exchange for news and views and it seemed an awful pity that, after the war, cars once again took over. In retrospect, I realise better than I did then what it must have meant to Unionist families like these when, not so many years before, people like my father had held out for, at the very least, an Irish Free State. But by the time I came to know them they had weathered that chapter and their attention was then taken up with the world war.

Commuting by train and tram from 'Carraig Breac' to Leeson Street had its problems. Amiens Street Station – or Connolly as it is nowadays – can be very long by the time you have run to the furthest platform from which the Howth train always departed, only to see it pull out as you got near it! And there you could wait for an hour-and-a-half before the next one came, trying to do some of your homework in a not very inviting waiting-room. So when it was decided that I should board at Mount Anville for my final two years of schooling, there were plus as well as negative factors in the arrangement. I would have to part company for a time at least from some good friends and face into a situation where it would be necessary to try to make new ones. But I would not have to run up those awful steps at Amiens Street (no escalators then) carrying bags of books and other impedimenta.

At Leeson Street I had been awarded a Blue Ribbon – more or less as a sort of going away present on my last day, I would think (this was the equivalent of a prefect's badge; something Maev had, of course, merited from the earliest opportunity). At Mount Anville this was to have ominous results because at the Voting for Ribbons the following December, Mother Bodkin, the celebrated and by then very elderly Mistress-General, advised that '... if any gel has held a Ribbon in another of our schools it would be usual to vote for her in Mount Anville, and Una O'Higgins has been awarded one in Leeson Street'. End of eve-of-poll message – nothing about my having worn a Ribbon for only an hour or two. I was horrified, but would have been even more so if I could have foreseen that after less than two more terms (acute appendicitis kept me *hors de combat* for most of the spring term) I would be Head of the School the following year.

I think that sudden catapulting into having to take responsibility for matters for which I had little or no preparation affected the rest of my life, perhaps giving me an impetus to believe that I am capable of tackling unforeseen difficulties or perhaps causing me to take undue risks. Mount Anville at that time was feeling the effects of the war, not merely shortages of fuel supplies and a certain rationing of food (although on the whole we ate remarkably well), but another malaise became more serious – the number of girls who held that they would not have been sent there at all, were it not for the war. The result of this, they reasoned, was that they didn't have to obey the rules of where they were. Some would have been in English schools, while others felt equally out of place because their fathers had made extra money out of the war situation and they had been sent to a school where they did not feel comfortable or at home. The net result of all of this was that in my year as Head, thirteen girls were asked to leave Mount Anville, something that I don't think had happened ever before! My anxiety became acute; the Head and the other Ribbons were expected to take some responsibility for the morale of the school, and my poor mother became the recipient of constant worried letters from me, although what she was supposed to do about it I don't know.

Another result of the war was that some very young children were then sent to boarding school, children whose parents were overseas and who had been sent home to Ireland for safety. So you might see tiny ones in flowered pinafores clutching teddy bears arriving in the Refectory for meals. No doubt it was some of those mainly country-women, whom we called lay sisters, who mostly minded them. Those sisters, with smiles that I remember strongly as part of the beauty and truth to be discovered at Mount Anville. Sister O'Neill, who had a little office in the 'wash-ups' or 'the fountains' (or 'the jacks'), who was said to be in constant pain with Meunier's disease but who got through an immense amount of mending and sewing and praying, was everybody's mother. No matter what your troubles, you could bring them to her and be sure of her care and concern. Apart from the inimitable Mother Bodkin (then in her eighties), the cool discipline of Mother White remains with me, but so too does the sympathetic twinkle in her eyes for a lame dog. Mother Clanchy's classes on Renaissance Art would equal any of Sister Wendy's (Mother Clanchy who, as Reverend Mother once said to me, looked as if she had been buried under a stone and dug up again), and only Miss O'Dwyer could have got me through Matric and Leaving Cert Maths. Altogether, there was beauty and truth to be found in Mount Anville, maybe not all day and every day, and maybe not for everyone, but I certainly retain happy memories of my time there, even though I do recall the stresses already mentioned. One thing I found especially stimulating was getting to know girls from places all around the country – something no day-school can offer. Thankfully Mother Bodkin, continued to smile on me in spite of the upheavals in the school, sharing her reminiscences about some of my grandmother's cousins who had been removed from Mount Anville at the time of Queen Victoria's visit, since no Sullivan could curtsey to a British queen! (I apologised to the shades of those cousins when, a few years ago at the British Ambassador's Garden Party in Glencairn, I said to Victoria's great-great-great-grandson: 'You are very welcome, Sir', but there was a lot of difference between their position then and mine now; and a handshake is not a curtsey – is it?)

Among the highlights of my memories of Mount Anville and of Leeson Street would be the torchlight procession on the 8th of December with the chorus of 'Immaculata' resounding through the candle-lit corridors and the frou-frou of our special white silk uniforms and white veils, ending with the offering by each girl of a lily – the 'lily of her heart' – at the fresco of Mater Admirabilis in the Lady Chapel. In summertime the solemn Corpus Christ procession seemed always to be held in sunshine in the grounds of Mount Anville. For it both schools joined together and it was attended also by many visitors together with choirs of priests and clerical students, while on Rogation Days there was a less public procession bordering the fields to ask a blessing on the crops and animals of Mount Anville's farm. In Leeson Street I remember especially the Christmas Bazaar, its stalls laden with home-made cakes and sweets decorated in green and blue crêpe paper (the Leeson Street colours; Mount Anville's were crimson and gold), while the perfume of hyacinths coupled with the glow of a lighting candle suddenly whisk me back to the little altars we could share with a friend during the days of the Annual Retreat. And oh, it mattered terribly if the one you thought was your special friend had decided to share with someone else, although in fact silence was the rule of the day throughout the Retreat.

In Leeson Street, too, when Mother Sheehan was Mistress of Discipline, on one day per week we were supposed to speak only Irish in the Refectory at lunchtime and on another day only French, while at Latin class with Mother Hogan, for a time we were supposed to say 'Good morning, Mother – dic, duc, fac, fer, dicite, ducite, facite, ferte', before she got the short distance from the door to her desk! Mother Hogan was a dynamic teacher, full of fire and energy, but she could be quiet too, like the time in English class I gave her my best rendering of Portia's 'The quality of mercy ...' and waited for what seemed an eternity before she breathed very softly 'exquisite'.

Somehow, when I left school I didn't seem to have the hankering that many of my friends did to go straight to 'College'; for most this would have meant UCD. Instead, I wanted something more broadening, as I would have seen it, and so I spent the following year attending Ria Mooney's recently opened Gaiety School of Acting and taking other classes in conjunction with that course: at the League of Health and Beauty with Kathleen O'Rourke; singing lessons with Jeanne Nolan; and piano lessons with Dorothy Stokes. All of these interesting women left lasting impressions on me, but none more than Ria, someone who I feel has never been sufficiently recognised. Ria, with her tremendous warmth, humour, talent, courage, with her sense of realism and sheer love of life, with her appreciation of beauty and her gutsy approach to everyday problems, ended feeling lonely, undervalued, unloved – I later learned. But at the time I knew her, subsequent stars like Milo O'Shea and Eamonn Andrews were just among her first year students and I remember the soul-searching before the latter decided to give up his office day job (at £3.50 per week) and turn professional. Others who took classes with her included Kathleen Ryan, P. J. O'Connor, Rita Foran, Bill Foley, and John (later Barry) Cassin (father of RTE's Anne Cassin). Some were mature students, some, like me, had barely left school, we came from very different backgrounds but she held a fascination for us all with her ability to transform the Gaiety Green Room from Pegeen Mike's kitchen into Lady Bracknell's salon just by the inflections of her memorable voice, the arching of an expressive eyebrow. Her Lyubov Andreyevna in 'Cherry Orchard', her Countess Cathleen, her Mollser in 'The Plough and the Stars' opened windows with panoramic views. Finding our way home afterwards on a rainy Dublin evening we felt challenged to absorb and to reflect some of the uplift, some of the outreach we had experienced. But she was in no way centred on herself; she could tell in a moment if a student was feeling poorly and make due allowance if their performance was mediocre that evening. Without interrupting the class she could soothe a headache with a gentle massage on the back of a neck. She had been at school in Loreto College, Stephen's Green at the same time as my mother, and there was a warmth between them so that once or twice she came to 'Carraig Breac' to stay for a weekend. On one occasion I spent a weekend with her at her retreat in the Dublin Mountains, where Roibeard O'Fearachan was another guest and where I listened fascinated to the two of them swapping views on literature, poetry and, of course, the state of theatre in Ireland at that time.

Ria in her youth had played the prostitute, Rosie Redmond, in 'The Plough and the Stars' and so could well remember the riots that had erupted around the Abbey at the time of its first production. While she was still young and playing juvenile leads, her glossy black hair began to turn grey so she hastened to dye it. It was later while she was touring the US with the Abbey Players that she came close to death from an illness for which no diagnosis was forthcoming and it was only when a specialist discovered that she was suffering from lead poisoning as a result of the black dye she had been using in her hair that she began to recover. The name Burgess Meredith fits somewhere into that story.

It seems that I, too, once had the opportunity of appearing in the Abbey. My mother told me that W. B. Yeats had wanted me, when small, to take the part of a child in an Abbey production of one of his plays (was it 'The Hour Glass'?) but that she had not favoured the idea. Also, she talked of my father and herself sometimes going on a Sunday evening to Yeats' home to hear him reading from his Noh plays (something I'm afraid she found boring due to the monotony of his presentation). His earlier Celtic period appealed to her much more and certainly, as I have said, for me, Ria's Countess Cathleen resonated in a manner never to be forgotten.

Describing the portraits in the Municipal Gallery, Yeats is perhaps less than flattering about my father, but his short poem 'Death' – said to be written about my father's death – is striking. However, the lines on the subject of O'Higgins which I find the most haunting are those by R. N. D. Wilson with which Terence de Vere White opened the first edition of his biography published in 1948:

> We thought this age of violence had found
> One man whose will had wrought a nation's peace
> And given to men that passion he had crowned
> With all the fearless intellect of Greece.
> Did we forget that Athens had not room
> Even under Pericles for those who best
> Had loved her that we had thought short of the tomb
> A mind like his could rest?

For my own part I was not sure that I wanted to 'go on the stage'. I only knew that beauty and truth had to be pursued and I was not at all certain that the rest of the professional world, to which I belonged, could deliver them in recognisable form. So I worked away with Shakespeare (as he never was at Mount Anville!), Shaw, Teresa Deevy, Kate O'Brien, Moliére et al., hoping that one day I would discover what was driving me. But when I was cast for our annual public performance as one of the three inhibited daughters in Lennox Robinson's 'Crabbed Youth and Age', there seemed to be a moment of truth, painful truth. The mother in that play was my mother – charming with lots of friends; I was in reality a shy, unattractive girl who would 'never be like her mother'.

However, life, as most of us know, isn't a straightforward path to truth and beauty, and one must soldier on. A party was held in the Gresham Hotel to which some of Ria's students were invited and I actually sat at a small table with the lovely Deborah Kerr, in Ireland to shoot some film. Subsequently we were invited to audition for 'Hungry Hill' then being planned by a company called 'Two Cities Films'. The audition was fairly harmless – did I give Mr. del Giudici a taste of my Countess Cathleen with the years like great black oxen treading the world? I can't remember and I'm not sure that it mattered; more likely that something in the shape of my jaw made me filmable and so I was to be offered the part that was later played by Kathleen Ryan under another director. With that the fat was in the fire at home! My mother and grandmother took to the 'blue Rosary Novenas', I'd say. Anyway, they were distinctly worried as to where all this was leading, so when the company went bust not long afterwards I was not altogether surprised! Some things just aren't meant to happen!

Subsequently I was invited by friends of the US Embassy to the Mansion House to a reception being held in honour of naval personnel in Dublin on a courtesy visit. Off I sailed in a long bouffant gown thinking perhaps to meet the sun-tanned man of my dreams, only to discover that, since my dancing classes had omitted teaching me how to twist or boogie, not many of the men there were too keen to partner me! Another celebration I was invited to because of my being a student of Ria was at Áras an Uachtaráin, where President Sean T. O'Kelly and his wife Phyllis were hosting a joint eighteenth birthday party for her niece, Una McCullough, and Princess Claudia von Hapsburg who, together with her brother Max, had been placed in their care by the then Pope Pius XII until their future was more secure. If I felt rather lost on that occasion (I knew hardly anyone there and, of course, had no idea that I would later marry a nephew of Phyllis O'Kelly), maybe the Hapsburgs felt a little lost also? And my spirits were not greatly raised by the solemn bronze bust of my father by Oliver Sheppard which stood in the room in which we danced, while Sean T.'s rendering of his party-piece, 'The Lark in the Clear Air', was a gallant effort but somehow didn't add to the gaiety of things. It must have been a difficult assignment for a childless couple like the O'Kellys to take on two imperial teenagers, but they were generous and hospitable and were always devoted to the young people in their extended family.

The news that I had been chosen for a leading role in 'Hungry Hill' broke when Maev and I were staying with a family friend, the Parish Priest of Glasson, near Athlone. Father Maurice Weymes lived in a very old-fashioned house with oil lamps, turf fires, and he produced wonderful musical concerts on his piano. Even when I was quite young he would stand me beside the piano and teach me songs such as Schubert's 'Serenade', 'Who is Sylvia?' and 'Du bist die Ruh', before embarking on Beethoven, Schuman, Brahms or Chopin. He still comes compellingly to my mind when I hear some of the music he played with such delight. But his was not the place from which to negotiate a film career – even if I were sure that I wanted one. Nowadays Glasson has moved smartly upmarket, I'm told, but at that time it held all the charm of a very distant rural retreat.

Maev in the meantime was privately investigating her own dream of beauty and truth in a very different way and had taken to stare into the fire at times, for all the world like a girl in love. And then she spoke her thoughts. She would like to enter the Carmelite Monastery in Blackrock – a love affair indeed, but an unusual one, especially for someone as keen on the academic career which until then she had been following with distinction. Could she not at least wait one more year and be called to the Bar first? Well, NO, she would prefer to go in a few months time. And so without fuss she made her preparations. At Carraig Breac it felt as if a foundation stone were being removed, but the accent was always on following God's will and the parting took place in great love and peace, although in anguish (a large tear rolling down Uncle Arthur's cheek after she disappeared behind the black grille). Later, at the Royal Irish Yacht Club in Dun Laoghaire, where he brought us for a much needed cup of tea, he tried to cheer us up by telling us that we'd better enjoy it since it was costing him over seventy pounds (he was adding up the annual subscriptions which he had paid since he had last visited the club). I never saw my mother weep, but for quite a time it felt as if a big slice of her were missing, and it was a while later before she drew consolation and strength from her Carmelite daughter's vocation.

As for myself, I felt a strange call to family solidarity and before long announced that I should like to become a solicitor's apprentice in Arthur Cox and Co.

Whatever about truth, there was little of beauty in lawyers' offices in those days, nor in the Civil Service offices where ghastly empty milk bottles might be the only ornaments, but the staff in Cox's were wholly welcoming to me and I enjoyed many friendships there on a strictly upstairs-downstairs basis. It was downstairs that the power resided in the sanctum of the boss; upstairs was for everyone else. I don't think I ever saw Mr. Cox upstairs and I don't think he would have recognised a number of his staff if he saw them. He ran his tightly controlled ship by a system of notes on the back of used envelopes (he was before his time in saving the rain forests) and only very few chosen people made it into his own office. Two secretaries who were sisters guarded the entrance to this retreat in adjoining outer rooms (my mother called them 'the alsatians'), and altogether there was quite a formidable aura of protection around him.

When I joined there were no other Dublin apprentices, although many who subsequently became legal luminaries had earlier served their apprenticeship there. Apparently at that time things could get a bit lively and out of hand so that one day a game of football in the room over Mr. Cox's head was interrupted by a plaintive note: 'Who let in the horses?' In my time the only other apprentices who were admitted were those of country agents such as V. P. Shields in Loughrea, Patrick Hogan & Company in Ballinasloe, Dillon-Leetchs of Ballyhaunis and Callans of Boyle. At times I would try to learn some law (I was apprenticed to D.J. O'Connor who lectured in the Law Society on the Law of Property and was also well-known amongst the rugby and sailing fraternity – someone I greatly admired but was much in awe of.) But I can't say I learned as much as I should have, mostly because, being already adequately staffed, they had no real need of apprentices.

When I was taken on it was understood that I would never discuss at home anything to do with the office and I more or less adopted a similar rule about not discussing Carraig Breac in the office. That way, things worked out successfully enough and I learned to be quite comfortable with my double life. The drawback, however, in belonging to such a big outfit, from the point of view of an apprentice was, as I have said, that they had little or no need of your services. Friends apprenticed in small one-person offices became more and more knowledgeable and competent while I idled and chatted or filled in forms or delivered deeds to various offices around the town. Calling a barrister at the Law Library was more exciting; there I would find a warm welcome if I had a brief for a not-too-busy practitioner. By then Uncle Tim Sullivan was Chief Justice and I was once called to his sanctum to be received by him in state. I cannot remember if I wore a hat on that occasion, but I imagine I did because women could never enter a court without one and I would have considered this as much the same. Never mind that as a child I had been encouraged by him to sing his ditties at the dinner table (though Maev had frowned on this, saying Mother wouldn't like it); now this was a Chief Justice receiving a very junior apprentice and proper respect was due, I would have felt.

In order finally to place 'Solr.' after my name I attended lectures in UCD twice weekly and others in the Incorporated Law Society where my 'master', Dan O'Connor, as I have said, lectured on Property. In UCD we never seemed to get further than Quia Emptores – a medieval Act apparently of huge significance but not of much use in the there and then. It was Declan Costello, a year senior to me, who kindly helped me to break the ice in 'College', otherwise it would have been an intimidating place unless one had the panache of 'The B.M. D.' (the Belgian Minister's daughter) who turned up for lectures with flowers in her hair and oozing attraction! My cousin Don O'Higgins, embarking on a legal qualification after some years in the Army, was in my year, although, being a few years senior in age, he sat a little loose to the idea of attending every lecture. Sometimes, if he were absent, I would answer the roll for him in what I judged to be an appropriate growl, sometimes if he were feeling a little sleepy (these were 9.00 am sessions) he might come to and answer my name instead of his own – Una being lower on the list than Donal. Since he was apprenticed to his brother Michael (a 'graduate' of Arthur Cox's but by then running a one-person office in Trinity Street) he got a lot of work to handle in his office, which I envied. At that time Don was also editing *Forum* magazine, which had earlier been started by his elder brother Tom, together with Alexis Fitzgerald. By the time I came to know of this Fine Gael journal subscriptions were waning and much of the material seemed to be written by O'Higgins's. Accordingly, when I dared to offer one or two pieces, I called myself Anne O'Neill, in order to make a change. Later, Don went on to a distinguished career in journalism, working for Reuters and for United Press. Other faces I saw at the Law Society lectures, which later became well-known, included those of George Colley , C.J. Haughey and Terry de Valera.

But the main way in which I learned any law that I did learn was through the Grind run by Brendan McCormack at the corner of Bachelor's Walk. There we packed tight as sardines in order to benefit from his clarity of presentation and the copious notes which he supplied. The air was thick; I don't suppose smoking was permitted during his sessions but anyway the air was thick, but it was essential to be there if you wanted to pass your Final. Another pathway to legal lore generously made available to me was through my cousin Tom O'Higgins, then at the Junior Bar. But he went further and undertook the most courageous task of teaching me to drive a car! Nobody at Carraig Breac drove (Uncle Arthur had desisted from the time he hit a cow on the road to Limerick) and gone were the days of chauffeurs, so it was essential for me to take to the road. Nothing can describe the goodness of Tom at that time. Once when I got my mother and an elderly cousin out to Maev's convent, I left them there and walked into Blackrock and phoned the Bar Library to tell Tom that they were there but nothing would persuade me to drive them home! I had had a near shave at Sandymount on the way out and was very shaken. Out came Tom to Blackrock to offer reassurance and encouragement so we finally got back to the Baily. On another occasion we were visiting my godfather in Naas, Father P.J. Doyle, P.P., when the wipers failed on a wet winter's evening and Tom came down to Naas on a bus to pilot us home. Moreover, since Uncle Arthur would not allow me to drive home on my own late at night after a dance, he would frequently enquire whether 'Mr. O'Higgins' would be there and, if so, that would be alright because Tom would tail my car ten miles out to the Baily before getting home himself. The big watchword in the clan at that time was 'standing in'; if ever someone stood in for me, Tom did, and I have never forgotten it. When he married his lovely Terry, I was thrilled to be a bridesmaid and lately was delighted to celebrate with them the Golden Jubilee of their wedding.

Being in sole charge of the Carraig Breac car was indeed a learning experience – and an expensive one for my stepfather! My driving lessons with Tom had mostly taken place in the Phoenix Park, where hills never seemed to be a problem and the handbrake was not much of a factor. It was another matter on the sloping driveway of Carraig Breac, however, where 'Hilda' the Hillman Minx lived up to her name and on TWO occasions sidled across the gravel and then gathered speed down a fairly steep bank before hitting the boundary wall below. The first time I had not thought much about the handbrake; the second time the brake had been well and truly applied but I hadn't known about leaving her in gear as well. Poor Hilda was somewhat shaken by these experiences but gallantly took to the road once more after a facelift and much repair work. Parking in Dublin then was tricky; fancy only being allowed twenty minutes at the top of Grafton Street, for instance! And when I tried to park outside Brendan McCormack's offices on Bachelor's Walk a young Guard stopped me: 'How long do you want to stay here? What time do you come out?' And when I did come out there he was at the doorway with another question: 'Are you ever free on Sundays?'

Occasionally, I would have to toggle between my humble apprentice mode and my chauffeuse mode so as to drive an important client somewhere, for instance if they were staying at Carraig Breac, as Gabriel Pascal, the film guru, did more than once. The Pascal episode created a major sensation in Cox's. Such was the excitement at the prospect of all the film rights of the plays of George Bernard Shaw being vested in an Irish company then being launched, that a suite of (it must be said rather dusty) offices in those premises was made available to Pascal's administrator, Michelina Buoncore. Occasionally, Mr. Cox took an early morning flight to consult with the great G.B.S. himself while Gabriel would assure my mother ('Breegeed darling') and myself that soon he would take down that awful railway line that spoils our beautiful Custom House and place it under the river instead. Others deeply involved in that romantic dream of Shaw's films coming out of Ireland were Johnnie Robinson, senior partner in Robinson Keeffe and Devane, architects, together with Eustace Shott of Craig Gardner's, accountants, and Father Cormac O'Daly O.F.M., Guardian of the Franciscan Friary on Merchant's Quay and chaplain to the Catholic Stage Guild. Being only at a very low level in the office I had little awareness of the business side of things, but at Carraig Breac Gabriel would bite into his raw carrots and wail about the 'leetle people with leetle minds' (who perhaps were the Cinema Owners Federation) who were not complying with the project. Meantime, he was casting his eye around to find an Irish St. Joan, but somehow failed to notice the angle of my jaw bone which had impressed Mr. del Giudici Not that I entirely escaped his attention – God bless my mother and stepfather's innocence – but I managed to keep things under control so that, at least on that score, all remained well. After some months of serious endeavour the project failed, the lights on one landing of Arthur Cox and Company faded and the curtain fell on a breath-taking might-have-been. Perhaps the only brightness now remaining is the brilliant yellow silk scarf I still retain, a gift from Gabriel bought in Walpoles over fifty years ago. At Ayot St Lawrence maybe an ancient sage was not too surprised at the fading of another Irish fantasy.

Around the corner from Arthur Cox's, in No. 16 Hume Street – the H.Q. of Fine Gael – I became involved in politics to the extent that I attended meetings where students updated and reorganised electoral registers. Arising out of that I found myself, rather like my sudden rise to stardom in Mount Anville, being entrusted with organising speakers for the Election campaign of that year, 1948. It says much for the state of the Fine Gael machine at that time (four or five full-time staff and everything else was voluntary) that this could happen. But it did and, taking a bit of a sabbatical from my legal pursuits, for several weeks I sat in Hume Street saying to one man (I'm afraid I cannot remember any women speakers) 'Go' and he goeth, and to another 'Come' and lo and behold he cometh. Even such as 'the General' (Dick Mulcahy) and my uncle Tom O'Higgins did my bidding and addressed meetings wherever I decided. Heady days indeed for which I was rewarded with an elegant pigskin briefcase! Naturally we were all thrilled (if a little stunned) when, after sixteen years of uninterrupted rule, Fianna Fáil was toppled by an Inter-Party Government led by John A. Costello of Fine Gael – an outcome I had never heard discussed before the election. It took a lot of getting used to; for all but my first five years Fianna Fáil had always been in power and my relations would look bleak indeed whenever Dev's rather lifeless tones were broadcast to the nation. Now here was gruff, shy but to me friendly Jack Costello (I often had stayed at the Costello's home after dances or parties) calling the tune instead. But, like most things, there was a downside also.

What was one to think of Sean MacBride as Minister for External Affairs? MacBride, who had been Chief-of-Staff of the

IRA and a prime suspect after the assassination of my father, was now sharing in cabinet with Uncle Tom and was a constituency colleague of my cousin Michael in Dublin South-West. But strangely I managed to surmount those problems more easily than another which I found even more difficult. It would be pretentious to say it had to do with the underlying programme in search of truth, but I couldn't quite square Fine Gael's subsequent policy on relations with Britain with what had been declared to be the party line before the election. Then there was emphasis on retaining membership of the British Commonwealth; had I not spread this message strongly on the hill of Howth (and Maev before me) so that they might not be tempted to flirt with de VALera's party? Membership of the Commonwealth had been one of the very few explicit policies which had distinguished Fine Gael from Fianna Fáil at that time, but before long John Costello was declaring the Republic. Yes, I knew that when parties go into coalition they cannot hold on to their own particular manifesto in every respect, and it was not as if I had then the foresight to realise that a time would come when Irish governments would be glad to forge much closer ties with Britain than mere membership of the Commonwealth in efforts to contain the desperate situation in the North, but I just felt confused and disillusioned and never afterwards belonged to any political party. Much later I served on a Commission of Enquiry into the Penal System under the chairmanship of Sean MacBride (others in that group included Gemma Hussey, Michael D. Higgins, Michael Keating, Mary McAleese and Fr. Mícheál McGréil S.J.) during which time he proved to be very friendly and hospitable to us all and would sometimes tell me how he had been pulled in on suspicion of my father's murder. Since we are at something of the same turning-point nowadays with regard to the respectabilisation of Sinn Féin, I wish I were clearer in my mind about how relationships with Clann na Poblachta were handled then. But I remain confused. I know the Ministry of Defence could not be trusted to a Clann na Poblachta member; no doubt there were other similar problems. Forgiveness at a personal level is one thing, but there is such a thing as prudence.

PRO PATRIA MORI

– Reflections on the Michael Collins film and the biography of Hazel Lady Lavery

It is no doubt appropriate
that each should make their own of him
now he has fallen.
Self-justified assassins celebrate,
proud colleagues elevate his name
on lofty cenotaphs.
His weeping widow tries
to comfort his small children,
his lover may decide
to save her story for a later day.
Biographers, historians, all have their say;
poets, painters, sculptors
must quickly add him to portfolios.
Grandsons will struggle to recall his dates
for school examinations
and an Oscar-bearing actor may reach the stars
on his broad shoulders!

Meanwhile, contrastingly, his generous bones
in patient, uncomplaining silence lie :
'Dulce et decorum est pro patria mori'.

CHAPTER SIX

From Carna to the Cote d'Azur

As well as these extra-curricular activities, I had developed a penchant for the ballroom of the Gresham Hotel and spent many late nights there supporting charitable causes such as the School Unions of my friends. Moreover, I could be found dancing elsewhere, such as in the Shelbourne or at Hunt Balls or in country clubs. One evening in Kilcroney was different from others, however. Instead of the crowded dance floor and busy hum around the bar at the far end of the room, suddenly I saw a coffin flanked by six brown candles in large black holders. And all was silent – no sounds of lively music or peoples' voices. This scene held for some moments and then everything reverted to normal. Club Orange being the height of my drinking in those years, I just put this experience down to being over-tired and said nothing to my partner. At the end of the evening when we had collected our coats, however he looked shocked. 'A man died here this evening', he said. 'He had just come in from a round of golf and was standing there at the bar when he dropped down and they couldn't revive him'. I think when I told him then what I had seen he was even more shaken!

The man in question was not someone I had ever met, but he was a well-known solicitor whose office was not far from Cox's. Nothing similar has ever happened to me before or since, but my mother used to talk of how, exactly one week before my father's death, she had been seized by such a strong conviction that he had died in Geneva (where he was attending a conference) that she went so far as to tell his mother that she feared he was dead. When, a week later, the tragedy happened, she felt afterwards that she had been better able to get through it and to do what needed to be done because of having had to deal with so much shock the previous week.

Another experience she talked of was how, during the months in which she was awaiting my birth, as she moved around 'Dunamase' she was sometimes surrounded by the sweet perfume of flowers in rooms which contained none. Years later, when we ourselves came to live in that old house, I suddenly remembered that story and wondered whether the house had been trying to comfort her in advance of her bereavement, while also responding to a new life which later would bring more young people there, and so continue to put heart into it by calling it home.

But I was talking about my dancing and too many late nights, so that when, in an unguarded moment I hopped into a Mass X-Ray caravan with some friends and had a picture taken, I suppose it wasn't altogether surprising that my news turned out to be not good. Not too bad either, but consultants affirmed there was a spot of trouble and the thing to do was to rest and to take lots of fresh air. So I went to Carna in Connemara by way of acquiring sufficient Irish to pass my Law Final, taking long healthy walks down the Mynish peninsula to a woman at the far end who would be willing to converse with me on a daily basis.

Getting to know Bean Uí Uaithne was something invaluable, unrepeatable. She spoke no English and I had only school Irish (mostly Munster) but somehow we made a real friendship. She could understand little or nothing of 'wireless Irish' either, she told me, but she had no such thing in her house anyway. In fact, she didn't have much at all in her house except what you might see on the Abbey stage as a set for 'Riders to the Sea'. Extras were the spent electric light bulbs found washed up along the shore which she had placed in some of her cups on the dresser by way of decoration.

The floor was stone and a half-door would be left open on whichever side of the house there was least wind. A grandmother, Mrs. Greene wore shoes only on Sundays when she would walk to Mass, but she was never shod when driving her three cows to the nearest bit of grass. She had been born on Inis Mór and all she knew of the mainland was Carna. Once I drove her to the next village, Kilkerrin – a major event for her. When my mother came from Dublin on a visit and called to meet her, the hospitality offered was very special – milk-tea (tea made upon milk instead of water). Sometimes himself might catch a fish and they had a few ducks – or was it geese? – who scratched around among the rocks, but I have seldom seen such dignity among so few possessions.

It was a serious crisis when her clock stopped – a clock you could have bought for a few shillings at the time in Clery's or Woolworth's. I offered to bring it to Galway for repairs when leaving my mother to the Dublin train (thinking that no-one would repair it but that I could buy a similar one there without difficulty). 'Galway?' – she looked vague, 'isn't that far away?' But then she brightened; she'd send it to her daughter Maggie in Boston – Boston, almost the next parish, where all her family had settled, all except Eileen, the youngest, who worked in the knitting factory in Carna run by the nuns. Galway she knew nothing about; it was westward to Boston that the lifelines stretched. So the clock was duly posted off to Maggie where, no doubt, the problem was dealt with.

Certainly at least one large parcel came from Boston during my time visiting Mrs. Greene. On returning from her one day, I passed the postman toiling towards her house on his bike with something very bulky balanced on his handlebars. Next day she was full of the present that Eileen had received from her sisters and brothers in America who had clubbed together to send her a (wind-up) gramophone and records so that she might be happy to stay home with her parents. As I listened, I had a vision of Eileen twirling alone to the latest American hits while, with luck, before too long I would be among my city friends again, obeying Jimmy Masson's baton in the Gresham Hotel.

But in spite of all the good Carna breezes, it took a year or two longer before my X-rays were given the all-clear, although the 'spot' was so small that it seemed to be a case of now you see it, now you don't. At times I would break the rules about resting and I remember a certain difficulty trying to explain to one of Fitzwilliam Square's best how it was that he had seen my photograph in the *Sunday Independent*, hatted fetchingly (I thought) at the Phoenix Park Races on the previous day.

As winter approached, it was said that maybe the sea mists at the Baily would not be therapeutic, so my stepfather encouraged a visit to the South of France for Mother and myself – she for two or three weeks, me for a few months. This would have the advantage of improving my French and I would have lots of time to digest the folders full of legal notes I would bring with me.

One problem that did arise, however, was money. After the war there was a restriction on taking currency out of the country, and £10 per person per week was the limit. Through his friend, Louis Jammet, the Dublin restaurateur, Uncle Arthur arranged that we could stay, on our way through Paris, at the hotel of his cousin, Hippolyte Jammet. Now, Hippolyte just happened to own a 5-star hotel on the Rue du Faubourg St. Honoré, where the top brass of the UN were staying and where, although the pension was being taken care of in Dublin, if you ordered something extra, like a bottle of Perrier water, it could be that your whole week's allowance might be blown. So we crept out to little bistros in back streets to feed ourselves and bought mineral water in the sort of small shop that wrapped its bottles in newspapers. It was a pity that my mother lost her nerve when crossing the brilliantly-lit marble foyer of our hotel and dropped a large, full bottle (glass of course, no plastic then) smack under the glittering central chandeliers. It was a pity, too, when, in the middle of the night I managed to hit the bell for the valet de chambre instead of the bedside light. In next to no time there was a discreet knocking at the door and a polite 'Vous avez sonné, Madame?' 'Don't breathe', hissed my mother, 'or it will cost all we've got!'

Uncle Arthur, being the sort of workaholic who never went anywhere except on business and then very infrequently, but also being a devotee of Agatha Christie and other writers of who-dun-its, thought that to have a good time in France it would be necessary to take the famous Train Bleu when travelling south out of Paris. And so two compartments had been booked and paid for in Dublin before we left, beautifully appointed, in which we were minded and fussed over by the attendant like children with their Nanny. After that nothing had been finalised. Tourism on the continent was only beginning to revive after the war and it had proved impossible at home to get advice about modest guesthouses on the Cote d'Azur, where the tariff would leave enough change out of £10 to have some spending money for the rest of the week. Instead, Maev and my grandmother were enlisted to pray that suitable digs would be found. After a day or two in Nice, where the Syndicat D'Initiatif was very doubtful if our need could be met at all, they came up with the suggestion that we try Beaulieu-sur-Mer where the Villa des Palmiers had recently opened and was very reasonably priced.

Arriving at the imposing but welcoming Villa, we couldn't believe our luck; fine, spotless bedrooms with balconies, very pleasant cuisine and a smiling Madame. Monsieur, with scholarly white beard, was a little more withdrawn and academic, but nonetheless his clear blue eyes could twinkle in a friendly way. Moreover, there were no less than four dogs, Airedales, very well-behaved except between 5.00 pm and 6.00 pm daily when they enjoyed an 'heur de folie' and went on the rampage around the house and large garden. Breathing sighs of thankfulness and ascribing our success to the prayers back home, my mother eventually took her leave, leaving me comfortably ensconced with M. and Mme. de St. Maur. The weather was lovely; I made friends with Joanna, a Dutch South African girl, and on Sundays I would take the train into nearby Monte Carlo, where I was just able to afford a ticket for the weekly concert given by that famous orchestra. But, after some weeks, unexpected war-clouds gathered again and, for reasons which now escape me, there was a scare about an invasion from North Africa. Another guest at the villa was advised by her friend, Captain Liddell-Harte (expert in such matters) that she should return to Belgium, and all along the Cote d'Azur foreigners headed for home. Joanna received similar advice from South Africa, and so eventually I was back in Dublin looking up my winter woollies.

Which is why I missed the formal congratulatory visit of the Communist Mayor of Nice to the Villa des Palmiers soon afterwards to honour 'Monsieur and Madame de St. Maur' for having preferred to become known as such, rather than as the Lord Abbot and Lady Abbess of their respective Benedictine monasteries in Belgium. It seems that during the war their communities, fearing for the treasures of both abbeys, had entrusted them to this couple who, together with a few members of each community, had set out for neutral Spain. But, somehow, one thing had led to another along the way and now the treasure had become the Villa des Palmiers and another house further up the coast where the remaining members of that party were living. The 'Nice-Matin' headlined the story with gusto for days: 'Monseigneur a preferré le titre de Monsieur' etc.

Moreover, it transpired that it was because of my mother's enthusiasm for the 'de St. Maurs' that all this had come to light. She had encouraged a little English lady whom she used to meet in the English Tea Rooms in the town to change her lodgings (where she was not happy) and to take the room at the Villa des Palmiers which would be vacant when she herself returned to Dublin. But the hotel where *that* lady had booked in for the winter was not best pleased and had instigated an enquiry into the antecedents of the proprietors of the Villa des Palmiers and whether they had the appropriate licence to receive guests at all.

In Carraig Breac when this news reached us we were stunned. So *this* was why Monsieur had talked to us frequently about Abbot Columba Marmion, the only other Irish person he had ever met (Dom Marmion had been his novice-master). So *this* was why he wore that large amethyst ring, why she carried that tall staff while walking in the town, saluting the children playing in the park, with a Reverend Motherly 'Bonjours, mes enfants'; why Bernadou, whom she called the 'trésor de la maison' worked such long hours and cooked so beautifully – Bernadou, who had run down tearfully to the train as I sat waiting for departure, to thrust into my hands a bag of mandarin oranges which she had just picked from the tree in their garden.

Strange are the ways of prayer! No doubt my mother knows, by now, the end of that story – how before many more years went by Madame repented but did not rejoin her former community, instead joining a more austere Order where, it was said, she gave great edification and died a holy death. Poor Madame, how she had loved her fairly modest comforts –

her beautifully coloured knitting wools and her cosmetics. Monsieur, who also became reunited with the practice of his faith, had died before that, but not before he had spent time in jail for tax evasion. He had joined an insurance company in Nice with little or no taste or training for it, I imagine, and had got out of his depth. Whether he was, as rumoured, a son of the King of the Belgians, I wouldn't know, but he was certainly an impressive-looking man, with a meticulous concern for my faith, insisting that I should return to the public library a copy of 'La Dame aux Caméllias' because Dumas Fils was on the Index and so I must on no account read him!

CHAPTER SEVEN

'O young Lochinvar is come out of the West ...'

         – Sir Walter Scott

Having this bother with my lung put paid to another scheme I had in mind around that time. Dublin was a difficult city to grow up in comfortably, because poverty was so very evident everywhere. Children frequently went barefoot in the streets whatever the weather, while in churches such as Westland Row or the Pro-Cathedral, young pregnant women listening to Lenten Letters more suited to theologians, would look very pinched and wan. So my scheme had been to offer some spare time to a group attached to the Little Sisters of the Assumption in Camden Street, a group of lay women who helped the Sisters in their work in the homes of the sick poor. Whether I would have been a help and not a hindrance is doubtful enough because, although I fancied myself as a dab hand with children because of my experience as a part-time helper in Fairy Hill Hospital, I knew nothing whatever about cooking. (At school I had had to give the time set aside for domestic science to extra grinds in maths and at home my mother seemed rather keen that I would not mess up the kitchen in case it would upset Mrs. Fuller). But one day I actually got as far as knocking on the door of the convent in Camden Street where, after some discussion, they seemed to think it would be a good idea if I came back another time. So I just continued to rattle flag-boxes for the Society of St. Vincent de Paul and for the Belvedere, Clongowes and Castleknock Boys Clubs. Certain streets in Dublin were almost unbearable in my youth; visiting a tailor in a York Street tenement was an O'Casey experience but with real-life smells to go with it, and I never knew how the pretty little dressmaker on the Quays kept alive, let alone turned out such attractive dresses from her cavern, which seemed to have neither daylight nor fresh air.

At long last, the day dawned when I passed my Law Final and was handed my parchment by the then President of the Incorporated Law Society in its Centenary Year – Arthur Cox. Furthermore, I became a member of staff of his office, a small space on a return landing with a beautiful mullioned window (similar to those at Carraig Breac), having been partitioned off to make an office for me. The house, 42 St. Stephen's Green, had once been the townhouse of the Ardilauns and still contained some of their lovely chandeliers, (festooned with cobwebs, but my one soon was shining). I can't remember much of what I actually did in that office but I do remember receiving £5 per week for my trouble and probably I got by somehow with the help of the secretaries, the clerks and the office boy. (By then I think the in-house scrivener had retired but before that, Mr. McBreen had sat on a hugh stool at his sloping desk laboriously writing out deeds in beautiful handwriting with a quill pen on parchment). All of these seemed to know so much more about law than I did and I soon found that mediaeval Acts weren't a whole lot of use when faced with a real live client.

Fortunately, for the sake of any such people, I remained in practice for only a few months. This was because of what the receptionist downstairs referred to as 'the man in the coat'. (She was young and pretty and had an eye for such things). It wasn't Lochinvar at this stage who had come out of the West, but Eoin O'Malley, possessed of a lovely tweed coat of Galway grey which had captured her eye. When, after a number of visits I broke the news in the office that I was engaged to be married, 'Oh, Miss O'Higgins', she pleaded, 'do say it's to the man in the coat'. And it was and, before long, we were being fêted and wined and dined all over the place, and so my legal career never developed.

What did develop was a measure of political ecumenism – coming from a largely Fine Gael experience to join a family which included Seán T. O'Kelly, then President of Ireland, his wife Phyllis Ryan, a sister of Eoin's mother Chris, their brother Dr. Jim Ryan and sister Nell, all strong anti-Treatyites (Nell having been a hunger striker during my father's term as Minister for Justice). True, there was also the Fine Gael leader, Dick Mulcahy, married to Min Ryan, among the relatives, but my father's relationships with him had been somewhat stormy. Before I had started to become serious about Eoin I sought advice from my cousin Tom as to what way the O'Malley family's politics lay. The year was 1952, almost thirty years after the Civil War, but it still mattered to me and I had to know. Tom clearly admired Eoin and so, looking suitably vague and gazing into the middle distance, he offered the opinion that he thought perhaps they favoured the Labour Party. And I believed him!

Our wedding took place on the feast of the patron of peace, St. Francis of Assisi, a golden day in October. The President attended and Dr. Michael Browne, the then Bishop of Galway, officiated. Carraig Breac was looking its loveliest and the day was so fine we were able to eat out of doors. I was so hot that my velvet gown – a creation of Nelli Mulcahy's – almost stuck to me, and our page boy, my godson, now a High Court judge, turned head-over-heels on the lawn. A day or two previously there had been a large reception in the Gresham so the wedding itself was quite small – only relations and close friends. Unfortunately, it had not been possible to attract all the uncles and aunts of both families – ecumenism making more sense to some than to others. Anyway, what couple gets everything right for their big day? We didn't have much time for regrets before dashing to visit Maev with our retinue, and then flying off to Paris and London. Behind us we left my mother delighted, she said, that I had joined a big warm-hearted family. She and Uncle Arthur had recently stayed with Eoin's parents in Galway – his father was Professor of Surgery in UCG – when they were attending a Law Society dinner, and they had all enjoyed each other's company. Also, it had been noted by my mother-in-law that her husband had taken to singing 'Una Bhán' around the house – so all was well

As might be imagined, the early days of trying to keep house, however, were not so good! What in heaven's name was a 'back' rasher or a 'gigot' chop? And why was I so exhausted by the evening time that it was a positive pleasure to go to a fund-raising meeting at the Mater Hospital, where Eoin was a consultant surgeon because it meant sitting down for a while. Perhaps I should have mentioned before now that Eoin had thought he should present himself to my mother in a formal way and to ask for her permission to marry me. When I told her of this project she became quite nervous, not knowing exactly what was expected on such an occasion. In the event, it seems he mentioned with some pride that he had been a consultant for one year and had made all of £950. Heavens! She wondered whether that would keep me in nylons but fortunately restrained herself from mentioning this aloud. But back to my early weeks of cleaning and marketing and preparing lunches and dinners and doing most of the laundry by hand until my kind cousin, Rosaleen Shanley, living nearby, insisted on including our wash in her washing machine. And then relations or friends might call for afternoon tea, which meant trying to hack slices off the remains of the wonderful wedding cake, iced in astonishingly intricate patterns of Limerick lace, designed and presented by Lyons' of Drogheda. We trod through shards of icing for days as a result of my efforts.

Losing our first pregnancy was a tremendous blow, but my doctor, Tim Healy, the cousin who had in my childhood rowed me in boats in 'Glenaulin', assured me that this happened to a very high percentage of women and was not a cause for undue concern. Sure enough, in 1954 Kevin, our first son, made his breathtaking appearance, in snowy January.

Because of the illness at that time of Tim Healy, a much younger doctor delivered Kevin, a man with strong ideas that, whatever else happened, Eoin's sleep was not to be interfered with when we went home. Eoin, who was working so hard during the day was not infrequently called out at night as well. 'Put the baby in the farthest room', said my doctor. 'Shut both doors and set your alarm clock for 6.00 am and feed him then'. And so began the inevitable division that mothers' face, torn between two sets of needs (not to mention their own needs as well!) We didn't quite follow the above instructions, but Kevin was the only one of our babies who didn't share our bedroom in the early months. Fortunately, he was big and healthy and we did have him in the NEAREST room with both doors wide open, and he had a fine pair of lungs.

To help me with Kevin and the housekeeping came Margaret McSharry from County Sligo, a small steady girl with a wisdom far beyond mine. She and her boyfriend were saving to get married and this they did the following year, settling in Coventry although forever lonely for Strandhill. After Margaret came Kathleen Devereux from Wexford, who had been with us at Carraig Breac and whose smiling face I was delighted to see. Eight years later I was even more delighted to see the face of her husband, a Detective Garda based at that time in Shankhill who, in a crisis, very kindly met Kevin off a bus and drove him up the mountain to our holiday cottage at Kattie Gollaher. This had been Kevin's first solo journey; he had been staying with a friend near Arklow where his friend's mother had put him on the bus to return home and I was to meet the bus at Shankhill. But somehow I managed to lock the keys of my Volkswagen Beetle inside the car and even rocks hurled at its window could not break open that sturdy piece of German handiwork. And the bus was on its way … Thankfully, in my desperation I was reminded of Kathleen's husband and Kevin was subsequently able to regale his friends with the story of riding in a real police car.

Since his days of being involved with Siemens-Schuckert and the Shannon Scheme, Uncle Arthur had been an admirer of German engineering and so 'Hilda', the Hillman, had been succeeded by what, I think, was the first Volkswagen Beetle Dublin had ever seen. So unusual was it that, wherever I parked in the city, a little knot of people would be gathered around it on my return. In Henry Street one day this attention made me so clumsy that I managed to drop its keys down a Corporation grating right beside the car door. But the days of chivalry were not dead, and a kind knight promptly rolled up his sleeves, went down on his knees, lifted the grating and messed around in all the gunge until he found the keys. (Ever since then I never park near a grating if I can at all avoid it).

A little over a year after Kevin's birth he was joined by Eoin Joseph. Kathleen, who was still with us, continued to smile even when both brothers howled or wept at the same time, impervious to each other's distresses. We were living in Argyle Road in Ballsbridge at that stage and had a sunny back garden where, before long, they learned to kick balls and to ride tricycles. At one time it became noticeable that small Eoin (whom we called 'Ojo') was reluctant to go into the garden alone, and the mystery was not resolved for a while, until I realised that the boy next door, in quarantine because of some illness, was whiling away the boring hours by wearing his green devil Hallowe'en mask at the window and enjoying the results on our fellow. A gap of three years separated Ojo from his next brother, Arthur, but only a little over a year separated Art from Chris. By the time these two arrived we were, perhaps, more relaxed parents. Eoin could never listen to a child crying for any length of time, and indeed neither could I, so infants would be brought downstairs and rocked by him as he read his medical journals, if no other help was at hand. But a near-crisis emerged in his study – strictly out of bounds for children – where, as a toddler, Art intruded and fiddled with a small tap on the central heating radiator so that dirty water spurted out over final exam surgical papers which Eoin and the visiting Extern Examiner had spread out on the floor the previous night for discussion. Fortunately, the situation was discovered in the nick of time while the papers were still legible.

By then, we were living in Eglinton Road, and I think it was Professor Arthur Mackey from Glasgow who was with us that year. Certainly I remember the two older boys standing on the doorstep there when he was taking his leave, with tears pouring down their faces; he had been so kind to them and brought them down to Donnybrook to buy sweets that they were grieved by his departure!

There were many memorable visits of Extern Examiners over the years but the most exciting was when the whole bottom of the house got flooded to a depth of about a foot or more and Professor Selwyn Taylor from London, a former Naval Officer, took charge of bailing out operations. The flooding arose from a cloudburst in a summer storm during much of which I had been seated with Mr. Kevin Kelleher, Headmaster of St. Conleth's School, being informed of a misdeed of Kevin's, then aged eight, who had written a four-letter word on the blackboard. As the reader will have gathered, my life had been very sheltered – no four-letter words floating around Carraig Breac – but I felt it would have been uncooperative to make this clear to the headmaster and to say I had never heard this word before and had no idea what it meant or where Kevin had heard it – if not at school – and please could I go home now as the storm seemed to be worsening considerably? Instead, I professed shock, horror and assurances of correction and then seized the opportunity to discuss a much more mundane subject – the small matter that both boys seemed to lose absolutely everything they possessed or to leave them in school behind them. 'Oh, Mrs. O'Malley', he said kindly, 'for doctor's children they are not too bad'. I pricked up my ears. What special mark did doctor's children have in his experience? Apparently, the children of some other consultants had even left their overcoats in the driveway for cars to roll over etc. 'Their fathers have to be out so often', he said understandingly, 'and are not able to lay down the law very much, you know'. Yes, by then I did know.

Regaining home through the thunder and lightning, I heard Nanny call from the top floor of the house. This was Angela Downey from Portarlington, one of Fairy Hill's nursery nurses, who cleverly had brought children and small dogs (can Pekingese swim?) up to the bedroom floor and closed the gate at the top of the stairs while, below in the semi-basement, John McLoughlin, the gardener, whose 'day' it was, thank God, was doing his best to turn the tide that was rushing in under the back and side doors at the same time.

In due course, the unaware and weary surgeons came home from the exams, mounted the hall-doors steps where nothing was amiss and, no doubt, were considering some refreshment, when I managed to summon enough breath to roar for them to come downstairs where I was struggling to salvage dining room furniture and other items from the embrace of the swirling dirty waters. You have to hand it to British naval training; in a flash the visiting professor was wading barefoot through floods, trousers rolled up, lifting and rolling carpets and instructing how to use the stirrup-pump which Billy Hederman, another surgeon, had suddenly appeared with. 'Ah, steady on there, old chap', said John – a saint of a man who did gardens in his spare time, but whose real job was nursing in Dundrum Mental Hospital – as he laid a kindly, restraining hand on this bare-footed stranger. I'm not sure what happened after that, but I DO know that the dinner party we had planned for that night had to be re-routed to the Gresham Hotel. I should add, also that St. Conleth's was a most happy school, and the Kellehers a wonderful couple who created a warm, family atmosphere not only for their pupils but for their parents and siblings as well.

Before St. Conleth's our boys had the benefit of Mount Anville's Montessori School, under the keen and devoted eyes of Mother Power, Miss Cashin and Miss Kelly. Mother Power, who was not infrequently 'astonished' at some of the carry-on of our chaps, and sometimes not only astonished but grieved, can to this day recall the individual temperaments and characteristics of the very many children who had been entrusted to her care. Joan Cashin, the first to coach our boys in rugby, had been a girlhood friend in Leeson Street, and Mary Kelly I had known in Mount Anville School, so they were like extended family. Only the other day, Sister Power, as she is called nowadays (or even Vera!), was remembering how Chris had insisted on pushing pencils down between the floorboards although she had warned him not to; how he would stop for a while and then blithely continue doing it. Nowadays, I watch him trying to prevent his own small children from making much the same experiments, with no greater success, and when I tell him about his own doings he is surprised.

Finbarr joined us in 1961, and it was well that he came, because otherwise it would have been a very sad year, with the sudden deaths of my mother (aged 63) in March and of Eoin's father in September. With considerable reluctance, the Cox's had recently sold 'Carraig Breac' and moved to a house in Shrewsbury Road a few weeks before my mother died. Moving house has never charmed me, although I have done it many times. It was in the course of our move to Eglinton Road, when I had insisted on doing many extra things, that small Chris had come into the world weighing only four pounds, and six weeks ahead of schedule. It was clear from my mother's last entries in her diary that *her* move had greatly disturbed her and she wrote of the continuing tramp of builders around the place – 'Will they never leave ...?'

When I think about my mother's death, nearly forty years later, something still closes up inside me so you will forgive me if I do not discuss it further than to say she never regained consciousness from a massive stroke and died after four days. She was just putting on her coat to go shopping with her niece, Helen Schofield, when the illness struck. They were to look at bridesmaids' dresses for Helen's wedding to Paddy Dempsey.

1961 also was the year when the International Society of Surgery held its meeting in Dublin, a huge undertaking in a city with, at that time, few large hotels and without conference facilities. Mr. T. C. J. O'Connell (Bob), mainly responsible for the organisation of that event, professed surprise when, by degrees, he noticed that a number of the ladies' committee had other events on their minds as well as the Congress of Surgery, although he had warned them a year in advance. But had he warned their husbands? It was my particular task to turn Newman House, St. Stephen's Green, into a Ladies Club for the benefit of the visiting women, especially those who had to be billeted quite far away in hotels in Portmarnock and Greystones and so would need a restful place in Dublin during the day. Accordingly, wonderful things happened to old '86' such as Irish Ropes laying a new carpet for us, and Brown Thomas putting up all sorts of delightful showcases and spraying the premises with their particular perfume, while of course we had masses of tourist information and brochures for on-going holidays etc. Why it didn't occur to me to have a small matter like a needle and thread in place I will never know, but when a bride, bound for University Church next door, felt something give in the back of her dress and her bridesmaid agitatedly enquired from the Ladies Club if we could help, do you think we had a needle to save her blushes?

It was that September that Eoin's loved father died. He took ill in Galway just when the tail-end of Hurricane Debbie struck the west coast, a time when haycocks might be seen wrapped around the top of telegraph poles and seaweed came up the waste pipe of the bath in their Salthill home. He died in the Mater a short time later so, when Finbarr arrived in December, there were only Granny O'Malley and Uncle Arthur of the 'grandparents' to admire him.

Already, my stepfather had embarked on the idea of becoming a priest and had begun to wind down his business commitments and to disengage from his office. Shortly he would move into the Jesuit House in Milltown Park and prepare for ordination. Eugene McCague, in his biography *Arthur Cox* in 1994 has chronicled much of this development. To it I would like to add my own sense of deep indebtedness to those Jesuits who helped to facilitate this astonishing dream, in particular to Bishop James Corboy, S.J. and above all to Father Frank O'Neill, his 'angel', both of whom so impressed Arthur during his time in Milltown Park that, after ordination, nothing would do him but follow them to Zambia. By then, each had come to understand and grow fond of this eccentric and exceptional character and Bishop Corboy bravely took him on in Monze where, it was said, he personally used to spray his room with the appropriate anti-mosquito preparation because he knew that Arthur's love of animals would prevent his doing such a thing himself!

It is only fair, too, to register appreciation of the vision of Archbishop McQuaid of Dublin, who first gave permission for the pursuit of this late vocation and who came to Milltown Park two-and-a-half years later to ordain the seventy-two-year-old seminarian.

Arthur's short time in Zambia was a very happy one; his letters to Maev and myself were full of enthusiastic observations about the people, their way of life and always he would send messages to the boys about the animals. He had baptised Iseult, our new daughter, before his departure. His death, as the result of a road accident ten months later, came as a terrible shock. By the time I heard of it he had already been buried, because, of course, things must be done so much more speedily there. Nothing would ever replace his selfless concern for, his devotion to, my mother and ourselves. After Mother's death his first words were: 'I only hope she was happy'. He used to agonise during her frequent illnesses. If, at first, I had found his odd dress and peculiar shyness hard to cope with, I developed an almost wordless rapport with him, as I have said earlier, and learned to value him greatly, so much so that I would even agree to do things like try on overcoats for him in Tysons' (men's outfitters) in Grafton Street, because we were approximately the same height and he himself would never bother. ('Is that your knee, Miss O'Higgins?' Mr. Murphy might enquire politely as he tried to pin a hem to the required length while I might be wearing one of my almost ankle-length 'New Look' numbers). Dear Arthur, buried far away, in a very simple grave, but wonderfully tended in his last days by Irish Sisters of Charity, the Order which he had served for so long as lawyer and with whom his physician father had worked for many years in St. Vincent's Hospital in Dublin.

It was not long before that that we had moved out of town to 'White Lodge' at White's Gate of the Phoenix Park, where our lives took on a whole new dimension. In a small house with just about enough bedroom space for the family, it proved impossible for them to lose quite so many things as they had done in the three storeys of 68 Eglinton Road. However, that didn't prevent the younger ones, anyway, from leaving things behind them almost everywhere they went (Art arrived home one day clad in his football gear, saying he had lost absolutely everything else), but at least there was in-house peace. And the main advantage of 'White Lodge' was its delightful garden in a wonderful setting, which provided a sense of being in the country while only ten minutes drive from the Mater and from Belvedere College where the boys, by then, were at school.

We had in the meaning welcomed a most important addition – Iseult, our only daughter – a determined small girl whose ambition to play every game her brothers enjoyed, developed so quickly that before she was three, she insisted on going with Finbarr to nearby Mount Sackville School

Another to join us for a year while we were in 'White Lodge' was a Biafran boy, Vincent Moneke. I had had a sort of dream of rearing for a while an infant orphaned by the civil war in Nigeria, and so was rather startled to be assigned instead eleven-year-old Vincent in long trousers! But things worked out well enough, mainly due to the kindness of the Jesuits at Belvedere (who included him in Chris's class at no extra charge), to the good humour of Chris and his friends and of the rest of the family, and to the sheer courage of Vincent himself. Rather in the same determined manner as Iseult, he would plunge into any pursuit he saw the other boys engaged in which included, to my horror, jumping off a high diving-board at Salthill in Galway with a large plastic bag held aloft over his head like a parachute and a cry to his football hero, Pelé, but with no knowledge of how to swim! However, he reckoned that if the ot hers could do it he could too, and by the time the holiday was over he was indeed swimming. Vincent was an experience for us all. I learned to be embarrassed at having only pink Band-Aids to apply to his black skin and to salute the gaiety with which he faced into our family. But on the night of his arrival it had been hard for him and I saw something which previously I had only read about – someone actually wringing their hands in silent misery, and I had had to do the only possible thing – allow him to go upstairs alone and give him space in which to deal with his homesickness for a while by himself before attempting to alleviate it.

ADVICE TO A GROWING GIRL

If you have the courage of Bernadette Devlin,
then steadfastly say what you know is true
and do what you must do
according to your conscience
so you will live at peace with your own mind,
though never finding ease
in your uncompromising life.

But I have settled for half-truths and smiled
and sat at laden tables
and lulled malaise about inequalities
by thinking 'What's the use?
What can one woman do
in seas of platitudinous hypocrisy?'

Yet now I know!
Yes, I have seen brave women in my day,
read Dervla Murphy's pioneering escapades,
watched Kennedy wives support those shattered heads and
        not give way.
(So in an earlier day it was accomplished in my own home).

But maybe one time too
these women were uncertain girls like you
who had to teach themselves to rise?
Oh maybe one day, Iseult, you'll surprise us so
and be the leaven in the midst
of our complacent dough!

– *White Lodge 1975*

CHAPTER EIGHT

'Since the wise men have not spoken
I speak that am only a fool ...'
– P. H. Pearse

It was during our time in 'White Lodge', in July 1972, that what could loosely be described as my more public life suddenly took off. After what came to be known as Bloody Friday had taken place in Belfast, I read in the papers that a protest picket was being planned outside the offices of Sinn Féin in Kevin Street where the public was invited to make their feelings known with suitable placards. Bloody Friday was '... when the IRA exploded twenty-two bombs in Belfast spreading mayhem throughout the city and killing nine people', to quote Jim Cusack of the *Irish Times* on the twenty-fifth anniversary of that horror. Amongst those killed was a mother of seven children, aged thirty-seven, and also Stephen Parker – the fifteen-year-old son of the Rev. Joe Parker, Church of Ireland Chaplain to the Belfast Mission to Seamen – a teenager, helping to move people away from a car bomb when he himself was caught in its blast. An uncle of his, Lovell Parker, was on the staff of Weirs', the jewellers in Grafton Street, where Eoin and I had chosen my engagement ring, was someone who had often assisted me when choosing presents for others and who subsequently became a member of the peace group set up in Dublin after the Kevin Street picket, called 'Working for Peace'. Rev. Joe Parker's own group, which emerged in Belfast more or less immediately after Bloody Friday – 'Witness for Peace' – placed on the agenda of us all an incisive question, the answer to which, twenty-five years later, is at last being faced as I write. That question became its hallmark – 'What Price Peace?'

In an earlier day my father, when drafting proposals for a Dual Monarchy scheme – and before him Arthur Griffith, who had considered the same – had realised that if we wanted peace we would have to be prepared to pay for it. In less than ten years, my father had travelled what some considered a horrifying journey, from heartfelt verses of praise for dead patriots to proposing that the British monarch be crowned in an Ireland, united and independent, as our Head of State.

When I was young, such an idea seemed to be embarrassingly passé, but later, as what were euphemistically described as 'The Troubles' greatly affected me, I began to see the point – peace will require a price to be paid by all and it will be a heavy one. Unless that point is fully absorbed and accepted by all traditions on this island, it matters not that the great and the good from around the rest of the world support what we hope is a peace process. The enthusiast gazing with misty eyes at the tricolour, the advocate of a Protestant province for a Protestant people, must both understand that peace will only be bought at a price that may well hurt. After a quarter of a century I don't yet know the answer to Joe Parker's question but I know that it still stands and awaits an answer.

Anyway, in 'White Lodge' I read about this protest, at that time knowing little about the North except for one trip to Belfast for an under-nine entry in the Belfast Feis. But I thought I knew that people must not be slaughtered in my name and, as I had no car available, I called a taxi, having hunted for something black from which to make an arm-band and having nailed a message to an old brush handle: 'You Don't Do This in My Name'. Having no previous experience of any such demonstrations, I remember saying to the driver that he might not be able to get into Kevin Street because a big crowd would be gathering there, but to leave me as near as he could. In the event, I think about twenty or thirty people turned up, none of whom I recognised at the time but with whom I went on later to found the 'Working for Peace' group, from which, a couple of years later, developed the Glencree Centre for Reconciliation (1974).

Protest picketing, in which I have participated on a number of subsequent occasions, has always been for me an attempt to enter into dialogue – a way of saying 'We are here with a very important message which we need to discuss with you'. At the very least, a letter is handed in, so something more is achieved,

I believe, than lamenting at home over terrible happenings. And it seemed to me as a mother of a young family, and moreover as someone who had lost father and grandfather through political violence and so had some understanding of the finality of death, that it was not really open to me to stay at home and hack out in the Phoenix Park as if nothing were happening. We had seen on television the awful outcome of the Civil Rights marches and had experienced in Dublin the burning of the British Chancellery in Merrion Square as a result of the killings on Bloody Sunday in Derry. What were we waiting for?

Talking with Sinn Féin was not then an easy thing to achieve and there was a formidable aura about that part of Kevin Street which was distinctly off-putting. However, I'm afraid I could only smile when people would say quite seriously: 'If you would arrange your demonstrations somewhere else other than Kevin Street, say Stephen's Green, I would join you'. The trouble about arranging a picket is, of course, that if you don't get a reasonable turn-out it can be taken that people largely approve of whatever has happened. I remember, on one occasion when only a very small number arrived, I found myself counting a pregnant woman as two. Another time when one of our more glamorous members enquired from an observing Garda: 'Why are those people across the road taking pictures of us?' he replied gloomily, 'Faith, when you wake up without your kneecaps you'll know'.

It was in the home of that member a year or two after the opening of the Glencree Centre that we held a meeting which was unexpectedly attended by four Loyalist activists, as well as by a Government Minister, quite unaware of their presence. No doubt we should have informed him but they had, they said, set out from Belfast before daylight and, in fact, we had been taken by surprise by their arrival and also, let's face it, we weren't all that keen to refuse them because one or two of them were rather large. So the meeting went ahead and the people on the hard chairs at the back of the room never met those on the couches at the front. What connection there was, if any, between their presence and the fact that our hostess found a bullet hole in her window and a bullet on the kitchen floor beside the refrigerator the next morning I wouldn't know. Probably someone out shooting rabbits ...

By then, as I said, the Reconciliation Centre had become established in Glencree. 'Working for Peace' had become immensely strengthened by the services of Father Frank Purcell (an Australian priest) who became its first Organising Secretary during a year's leave of absence from the Society of St. Columban. So he was part of a delegation which, as a result of our pickets, held discussions with some Sinn Féin members – Seán (brother of Ruairí) O'Brádaigh, Joe Cahill, Aindreas O'Ceallacháin and one or two others. What remains in my memory is their total conviction about the justice of the Republican cause, no matter what means were used to progress it. Frank was struck also by the theoretical correctness of their grasp of the theology of a 'just' war but, when he questioned whether all the conditions for this actually existed, and pointed out that by then this teaching was undergoing serious reconsideration anyway, they did not want to know. At least some of these men were very religious and their youngest member was a teacher in a nearby religious school. Undoubtedly, a man of courage and commitment, he would deliver graveside orations for deceased IRA members at Milltown Cemetery in Belfast with the blades of hovering helicopters practically combing his hair; it was nevertheless painful to consider what kind of message he was passing on to the young in that school.

I also remember the ease with which they dismissed any problem that might relate to reconciliation with Unionists after the British might leave. Their leading member, with a strong dose of 'Some-of-my-best-friends-are-Protestants' syndrome, explained that in his home town of Longford his next-door neighbours were Protestants with whom he always had got on very well indeed. Was his mind REALLY as simplistic as that, or was it just that he thought ours were?

I think the first time I personally became fully aware of this equating of religious labels with political ones was in the corridors of power in the British Ambassador's residence in Glencairn. I had come to collect Sophie, our Pyrenean Mountain dog, which Sir John Peck and his wife had hoped to adopt. Sophie had become incorrigibly averse to the charity walks which frequently passed White Lodge, and she also greatly disapproved of motorbikes, so we were at our wits end about her. The hope was that in Glencairn, where she could not escape onto the road without foiling the Garda presence at the gate, she would exercise her charms and delight a hard-pressed ambassador and his wife without danger to the public. But I insisted that she should go first on trial; they already had more than enough problems on their hands! So she went to stay with them for the Hallowe'en long weekend. All would have been well, thought Sophie, if only the security of the place had been left entirely to herself. What possible need was there for the eighteen Gardaí patrolling the grounds by night when she was capable of handling the whole thing alone? And so from their bedroom window (she was *never* allowed upstairs in White Lodge) she roared these and other questions all night at the guards without ceasing. Neither did she approve of the small terrier belonging to the butler, so it cleverly turned a large flower pot over itself and went missing for hours, while Séamus McGrath's horses in an adjoining field got a taste of her presence also.

At that time, since the Chancellery had been burned down, officials had to work in the ambassador's residence where even the corridors were stuffed with desks and work tables. And it was as I picked my way through these, wondering how the pale, butter-coloured carpets would have stood up to much more of Sophie's enormous paws, that I kept hearing conversations about 'Protestants' and 'Catholics', where I would have always referred to 'Unionists' and 'Nationalists', or 'Republicans'. Some say it was the British themselves who applied this shift of emphasis, it being presumably more agreeable to try to deal with the religious wars of other people than with their contesting claims about the sovereignty one represents. But is it only the British who think that way?

On the theme of how essential it is to differentiate between faith and politics (a theme which was the main focus of the document which I later had the privilege of writing and submitting personally to Pope John Paul II), I have become quite allergic to the custom of soliciting the views of religious leaders on matters which are political. No doubt there was a time when Catholics were under-represented politically and so it was necessary for priests to speak for them, but why, when the SDLP and Sinn Féin and Alliance and the Women's Coalition and, indeed, the Unionist parties exist to express the views of their Catholic constituents, should it be thought necessary to find out, for example, what is the opinion of the Cardinal on the latest speech of the Secretary of State? Moreover, sometimes the political unawareness of the saintly can be disconcerting. If ever I have met a saint, I met one in Dom Helder Camara, Archbishop of Recife, yet something he said in Derry to a congregation of devoted people hanging on his every word greatly dismayed me. He had come onto the Irish scene as the guest of Catholic Episcopal and lay groups. His demeanour was the humblest, most Christ-like thing that I had seen; he wore no rich vestments, carried only a wooden crozier when, with all the faith that was in him, he assured those Derry people who had endured generations of unemployment and political heavy-handedness: 'THIS is the TRUE Ireland, people gathered as you are around the Mass altar'. Perhaps I might not have been so sensitive to his statement were it not that outside that church the previous week a young British soldier had been beaten to death in broad daylight, and it was with the weight of that recent death in their area that these parishioners had hung up their bunting in papal colours and unfurled their flags to extend a heartfelt welcome to this exemplar of non-violence. By then, I personally had come to realise that while being a Catholic was a very wonderful thing in itself, it had really nothing to say about being Irish, and the converse, of course, should be equally true. In fact, as St. Paul has taught us, in Christ there is neither Jew nor Greek, neither 'prod' nor 'téig'. Once in Corrymeela at a meeting of the Politics of Forgiveness Group, we each contributed a verse to the hymn 'He's got the whole world in His hand', the one I most remember being 'He's got the Pope and Paisley in His hand'. And we went on to adapt the story of the dove returning to Noah with an olive branch in her mouth so that an Irish dove returned with a small sheaf of poppies and shamrocks instead.

But somebody, somewhere – and preferably not a fool this time – will really have to see as their mission the careful separation of Irishness from Catholicism as a real contribution to the Peace Process. 'Are you a proper *Catholic* at all?' an irate Republican coming out of Sinn Féin Headquarters in Parnell Square in Christmas week, 1988, spat at me when I protested in the street there about the IRA terrorising the wives and children of British soldiers stationed in the North so that, together with their pets, they all had to evacuate their homes 'in the mouth of Christmas'. In Christmas week 1980, when a colleague in the peace movement and I had a private audience with Pope John Paul, I tried, as I have said, to state strongly the necessity to separate Catholicism and Irishness so that the integrity of each would be the clearer. When Nationalist and Republican children in the North had seen on TV British children waving their Union Jacks to welcome the Pope to Canterbury, they were hard put to know what to think – only the tricolour being suitably Catholic in their experience. The Union Jack was a negation of their faith. But I'm jumping too far ahead now; let's keep with the 1970s for the moment.

Before 'Working for Peace' finally made the decision to open the Centre for Reconciliation at Glencree, we gained a certain amount of experience, on a much smaller scale, by organising visits for Northern guests to Newbridge, County Kildare, where Irish Ropes had generously lent us their Staff Hostel. People came who were in need of respite from bombings and threats and we mixed the groups so that many of them were meeting members of another denomination for the first time. Saidie Patterson O.B.E., a veteran Trade Unionist and leader of 'Women Together', gave courage to many Protestants (hearts in mouths) to come south where they were amazed at the welcome they received. The opposite side of that story is that of an elderly Catholic lady from Newry who clutched my arm to drive home the point that she had been rescued from her bombed house by a PROTESTANT!! If it had been a dinosaur who had saved her she could hardly have been more astonished! Sister Anna, an Anglican nun in Belfast, also organised many to come south to us, and the Keadeen Hotel in Newbridge put up tasty dinners which a team of local ladies faithfully delivered daily, while a local doctor kindly looked after the health of our guests without charge.

Garret FitzGerald, Minister for Foreign Affairs, had opened our hostel and greatly encouraged us. For me personally this was a link with the past, since our fathers had been friends and colleagues and it was his father who had kindly brought Maev and myself to visit Leinster House for the first time. (This had been a big day indeed; I was nine and I wore my new red linen dress with large white daisies on it, and I was greatly struck by the blue-grey Dun Emer carpets with their borders of Celtic design. I remember too the sunshine beaming into the Seanad chamber where I noticed Sir John Keane, a family friend, having a quiet after-lunch snooze).

By the time that year in Newbridge was over we had more experience of working in a group and had a somewhat better idea of what might be involved if we opened the centre at Glencree.

Probably everyone who has ever participated in a voluntary group has wondered, at least occasionally, how much longer can they withstand the wear-and-tear of it – the endless meetings, the inevitable and not infrequent friction, not to say conflicts! But groups can be very valuable and the people who really deserve sympathy, I imagine, are those who suddenly find themselves in positions of leadership without a structured group behind them. I think of Mairéad Corrigan and Betty Williams, who had to form the Peace People around them *after* they themselves had hit the headlines; Susan McHugh and Fran Banks would have had a slightly similar experience in Dublin in Peace '93, although, of course, to a lesser degree. In contrast to such rapid developments, the Corrymeela Community had been studying and praying together for several years before they opened their wonderful Centre at Ballycastle in County Antrim, and we in 'Working for Peace' had over two years preparation before taking courage and signing on to open the Centre at Glencree and our office in Harcourt Street. By then we were becoming a little known, at least in certain circles, and we were glad to receive advice from any who wanted to see our work progress.

Sheelah Richards, whom I had often admired on the stage of the Gate Theatre and who was, by then, working for RTE, was one who would call into the Harcourt Street office from time to time to give encouragement and lend a hand. Pamela Hinkson, daughter of the poet Katherine Tynan and herself a writer, invited me to tea to deliver a warning. 'I have travelled a lot', she said, 'and lately I have been asking myself where else have I encountered an atmosphere similar to this one in Ireland today, and I am shocked to say that the answer is in Germany in the '30s – just before the war. Everybody', she continued, 'getting on with their own affairs. Women shopping, cooking, getting the children's teeth straightened and seeing that they passed their examinations, men keeping the head down and progressing their businesses, so that they were all a push-over for the Nazis when the time came'. I felt I knew what she meant but was unable to resolve the problem.

In the 1970s it seemed as if terrorism might take over in the North and even in the South, but that, as well as being busy in the ways Hinkson described, ordinary people did not much like standing up in counter-witness because they said it was 'political'. Organised bodies from the most august to the most basic were very slow to be seen to protest about the violence or to be in any way 'political', and even individual members might feel they had to lie low also, for fear of implicating their group. It was a question of priorities, it seemed, and one's foremost loyalty was to the organisation which had to be preserved no matter what, and which must not be put at risk by any taint of 'politics'. Also, there are some orthodoxies which can only rarely be confronted and some priorities which will prevail to the last. A good example might be a certain Saturday afternoon in Dublin when Betty Williams, still reeking of the smoke of the burned-out La Mon restaurant in Belfast where many people had died and been injured during the previous night and where she had spent anguished hours on her way South, led a Peace March in Dublin for which the turnout was not at all large. 'Did she not know better?' the wonder was 'than to come on the afternoon of an international rugby match?'

The project at Glencree was, of course, immense for a small group such as ourselves, but we tried not to allow it to consume all our energies because peace had to be worked for both in the short as well as the long term, and Glencree was then, and still is, essentially a medium- to long-term educational project. Building bridges and reducing prejudices takes time and can be slow work. Meantime, we wanted to keep with the needs of the moment as well.

So 1974 also saw us, in association with other peace groups, arranging Walks of Remembrance in Dublin, one which wound from Leinster Street to Parnell Street to mark the shocking loss of life in the bombings there:

> On Saturday they carried flowers to Leinster Street
> to ease the pavement agonised by blood
> I read your meaning, messengers of beauty
> when hate has done its worst there remains love

At Christmas time (again with the help of other groups such as Pax Christi, Peace Point, the Ballyfermot Peace Corps and Voluntary Service International), we managed to assemble 20,000 people in Merrion Square for an inter-denominational Prayer Service for Peace. This coincided with the Feakle Talks and we liked to think that the subsequent nine months ceasefire of the IRA had been assisted by the turnout of those thousands and the fervent prayers offered in Merrion Square that Christmas.

During the abduction of Dr. Tiede Herrema, members of Working for Peace and others prayed together nightly outside the GPO for his safety and it was a source of great joy and encouragement for us when he emerged intact from his long ordeal.

In March 1974, during our first annual Peace Week, the Reconciliation Centre at Glencree was opened, although not yet ready for residential habitation. 'Peace WEEK' exclaimed one Dubliner when she saw our posters going up. 'They don't want much! I'd give me two eyes for even half an hour of it!'

CHAPTER NINE

'It is better to light a candle than to curse the darkness ...'
– often quoted by Rev. Ray Davey, founder of Corrymeela

Our fright, even up to the last minute, about signing ourselves into the Glencree project was considerable. The decision had not been unanimous and the undertaking was formidable; those old buildings – vast, derelict, forbidding – were not everyone's choice. Why not, for instance, that cosy convent for sale in another part of County Wicklow with its comfortable cats snoozing in the sunshine and its box-lined pathways leading through sheltered, well-kept gardens? But the drive up to Glencree was reviving, challenging, uplifting and the views of the valley were breathtakingly beautiful and the belief grew that the terrain itself would somehow engender new hope and a vision of life's possibilities in people too long beset by political intransigence and by the curbing of their gifts. The beauty there would elicit truth, we believed.

'RESPECT' was the theme of our 1974 Peace Week – something which to me at first seemed rather tame. But as Frank Purcell developed his creative ideas about how that theme might be emphasised all round the country, I began to light up. We could encourage people everywhere to try, during that week, to show appreciation for similar groups or individuals with whom they normally had no contact by inviting them to some get-together, no matter how modest. Quite a good response resulted and in later years we marked the week with Walks of Remembrance in which we tried to cross a number of divides. Amongst those who led our Walks of Remembrance were General Seán Collins-Powell (a nephew of General Michael Collins), by then retired from our Army, who laid a wreath of shamrocks at the Memorial in St. Patrick's Cathedral commemorating those Irishmen who had fought and died in the World Wars of this century while serving in *British* forces. General Collins-Powell took up our invitation with heart-warming enthusiasm, saying it was something he had long wanted to do, but had been precluded from doing while still serving with our Irish Army. (Sad old world?) Another who likewise laid a wreath at that memorial in St. Patrick's was Seán MacBride, one time chief-of-staff of the IRA. Because of such initiatives Glencree was encouraged by backstage murmurings from Iveagh House to put out feelers about possible Army representation at the Annual Poppy Day Service in St. Patrick's – but without success. What did emerge, however, for the first time was official British representation at the annual Commemoration Service held at the German Cemetery at Glencree where the British military attaché in uniform laid a wreath of poppies in remembrance of the German dead, and everyone crossed over the road afterwards for a hot cup of tea and a get-together at our Centre for Reconciliation.

Others who led our Walks of Remembrance together were the Presidents of Ogra Fianna Fáil and of Young Fine Gael (grandsons of Seán Lemass and of Kevin O'Higgins respectively) who jointly laid a wreath of shamrocks at the Four Courts to remember together all who had died in the Civil War, while Cyril Cusack and Siobhán McKenna gave readings at the GPO in memory of all who died in 1916.

Socialising among friends not involved in the peace movement often presented problems, I found. People would be polite, even admiring: 'Aren't you GREAT to be so involved?' – but I couldn't help feeling they regarded me as somewhat bizarre. Praying for peace would seem to be alright and contributing to funds such as the Glencree Peace Bonds would likewise be acceptable, but often the feeling seemed to be that what happened in the North was mainly a problem for the people up there. (Never mind certain Articles in our Constitution having any pressurising effect and forget about caches of arms or training for the IRA or safe houses in the Republic). Inside the peace movement, however, where at times things might be far from sweetness and light – contrary to public expectation – at least we were surrounded by each other's awareness that the North was a tragedy to which we all belonged and our shared conviction that it was not only reasonable but that indeed it was our duty to do whatever we could to lighten the load.

Before long, of course, we learned that our task was not so much to sort out the North's problems but rather to comprehend better what a peaceful island might mean – 'What Price Peace?' What price will I pay, what am I willing to give up so that others may live in peace?' In St. Anne's Cathedral in Belfast Rev. Bill Arlow likened the situation to a number of people trying to complete a jig-saw puzzle while some will not give up the pieces which they insist upon holding close to their chests. From Rome, Pope Paul VI had proclaimed the same messages with his insistence on the maxim – 'Peace Begins With Me'. Never mind the faults of the other parties, take a look at your own prejudices, your own negligences. In Brazil, Dom Helder Camara encapsulated the path to peace in his little poem:

> If you disagree with me
> You have something to offer me ...

So in our Centre for Reconciliation at Glencree we were attempting to digest and to reflect such teachings; to learn with Paolo Frere that the oppressor too had to be loved and respected in a way that would liberate him from his oppression, and not to distil hatred against him while seeking to liberate the oppressed. We knew we needed many important skills – to LISTEN, LISTEN really well, and to think inclusively.

The premises at Glencree had been leased to us for a peppercorn rent by the Office of Public Works who, for a number of years, had been using it as a storage place for the antique tricycles, telegraph poles and other unwanted impedimenta of the Department of Posts and Telegraphs. The part of the complex at Glencree which we restored was that section which had been used as a school by the Oblate Fathers. The former British Barracks, gaunt and empty, was open to us at that time, also, but we could not attempt to restore it and only used it occasionally for work-campers and others who delighted in its rugged mystique. It had last been used as a hostel for German and, I think, French children who had been sent to Ireland immediately after the war for rehabilitation and who were cared for there by the Irish Red Cross and by some members of the Daughters of Charity. Recently a grand reunion took place at Glencree between many of those 'children' and the families who had fostered them from there – several hundred happy people swapping memories of what 'St. Kevin's Hostel' (the old Barracks) had meant to them.

At Glencree's inception, since we were an inter-denominational group based on the Christian concept of reconciliation, we attended each other's churches together for some time before, at that level, things began to fall apart. The early Glencree Council also included representation from the Peace Corps, Voluntary Service International, Peace Point and Pax Christi. The Peace Corps had originated in the R.C. parish of Ballyfermot, an organisation for young people which quickly spread to at least fourteen other Dublin parishes. This input from youth was immensely stimulating for us. I remember a small girl from Ballyfermot in frilled ankle socks gazing out at the valley (something she had managed to do by standing up on some heating pipes) and marvelling – 'Do you mean we can come here whenever we want?' Who could forget the generosity of that Corps with their constant enthusiastic work-camps and their gift to us of a large sum of prize-money which had been awarded to them? 'Glencree has been my University of Life', Rosaleen Walsh, an early member of that group and later a member of the Glencree Council has said. And it was mine as well.

After The Bombing of Horseguards Parade

– Set to music and recorded by The Wind Children of California

Sing a song of London with sunshine in the park
But centuries of hatred will make that sunshine dark;
Sing a song of London while horses' hoofbeats ring
But twisted hearts and twisted hands
Have only death to bring.

CHORUS:

Did you not bring a new song 2000 years ago?
Remember, Lord, that new song? How did the lyric go?
Did we not hear that new song that you were sent to bring?
When shall we understand it? When shall we start to sing?
'Children, love one another;
Brother, forgive your brother'.

Sing a song of London and children in the park
But we have taught them hatred to make their sunshine dark;
Lord, there was once a new song that you were sent to bring
But we have lost the music, teach us how to sing!

Work-camps were a revelation – not least a group of one-hundred-and-fifty Californians who managed to achieve in three weeks what the OPW had assured us would take up to a year, *viz.* they cleaned the three ponds, or small lakes, which fed the stream that had turned the Ferris-wheel to make electricity for the Oblates in their day. The wheel was still in working order, an expert assured us, but the ponds and stream had become blocked. What was needed was to free the water. And so the Californian 'Wind Children' (named after the Holy Spirit) tackled the problem with tools and camping equipment lent to us by the Department of Defence (after which they could claim to be children of water as well as of wind).

Actually, they were entertainers as well as work-campers – something along the lines of 'Up With People' – and I was very complimented when they put to music some lines I had written in the aftermath of the London bombings on Horseguards Parade. When they sang and recorded this piece I hardly recognised it, so professional did it sound with the contrasts of light and shade and the clip-clop of the horses' hooves all expressed in their singing.

I remember, too, another work-camp led by a perhaps over-enthusiastic Yorkshireman who was stressing his leadership rather a lot. 'B ... y Pommy', breathed our Australian Organising Secretary gazing at him out of the window before remembering 'Respect' and ruefully asking our pardon! I remember Ellen from the American mid-west working high up on the roof of the Forge/Prayer-room and Antoinette waking in the old Barracks one morning to find frost crackling in her hair. I think of James McLoughlin and his incomparable wife Sarah and the dedicated work they put into that place. And I remember the screams from the Barracks when, after ghost stories before bed-time, our young St. Bernard dog, Glen of Glencree, managed to make his way up to the girls' dormitory in the darkness and to lie down in one of their beds! Glen was an early companion to Father Shaun Curran S.J. of the Milltown Park Community, who came to Glencree as its Centre Director and whose delicacy of feeling concerning Glen's sensitivities did credit to his qualification to be a peace worker. Glen had a kennel beside Shaun's caravan where, regrettably, during the night his snoring proved all too audible to Shaun. However, the Director would only move the kennel away from the caravan one inch per night so that Glen would not be offended by the separation. There are prices to be paid for showing respect for, and appreciation of, the 'otherness' of the other!

'Working for Peace', which had been chaired by Dr. Ivo O'Sullivan, had made way for this larger support group for the Glencree Centre for Reconciliation. In joining the Steering Committee for Glencree, Eleanor, Countess of Wicklow, brought with her the goodwill and support of a great many women's organisations who had come together under her chairmanship as the Women's Voluntary Association, among them the Irish Countrywomen's Association, whose hand-knitted blankets still adorn the Glencree Centre today.

However, before long it seemed that the inevitable track to the US had to be trodden, or rather flown, in search of supportive dollars. In January '75, together with Dorothy Tubridy and Frank Purcell, I found myself gripped by the iron-cold of Boston streets in between broadcasts to what our Consul there, Carmel Heaney, described as a lace-curtain Irish listenership. Our message was not the usual Irish one as we strove to put it across that respect and understanding of those who differ from us is ultimately more important for Ireland than a thirty-two county Republic.

In New York I slept one night in Senator Edward Kennedy's bed (I have to say in his absence). In Pittsburg Tony and Susan O'Reilly not only put us up at their home but also hosted a large dinner party there for us, at which Tony spoke about our new Centre in County Wicklow and encouraged support for it. A few months later when Glencree made a second visit, this time in company with Doctor Barbara Stokes of St. Michael's House (a former neighbour at the Baily), Lady Valerie Goulding of the Central Remedial Clinic and Professor Bill McGowan of the Royal College of Surgeons in Ireland, Judy Hayes and Shaun Curran came instead of Frank Purcell and we were all present at a rather early breakfast meeting which turned out to be the inception of the Ireland Fund of America with its motto of 'Peace, Culture, Charity'. We were the founder members.

From a personal point of view, one particular experience in New York comes to mind. I had been given an appointment with the Honourable Paul O'Dwyer, at that time President of New York's City Council, in order to explain to him about the movement for Reconciliation in Ireland which was being undertaken at Glencree. Paul O'Dwyer's views were known, of course, to be strongly in favour of a United Ireland, to say the least, and I did not think he was much switched on by whatever I was saying until suddenly he fixed me with an intent look: 'Are you related to Mrs. Patricia Kirby of Kiltimagh because, if so, I must pay great attention to you?' Yes, I was indeed a niece of gentle, understated Patricia who, as a girl, had been a member of Cumann na mBan, who had been the daughter who struck the gun out of the hand of one of her father's assassins and confronted them before speeding several miles into Stradbally on her bicycle in order to summon a priest and a doctor. Whatever had passed subsequently between Aunt Patricia and Paul O'Dwyer at Kiltimagh in their shared concern for disabled people, he had considerable respect for her. And he went further: 'There is someone else here', he said, 'whom I want to listen to what you have to say' and he produced a curly-haired, fresh-faced young man from the next room. Whatever way I had misread the situation up until then I thought this newcomer was being brought in because he was a moderate, largely in agreement with my point of view, but it turned out that the senior man was the more moderate while the younger, gazing out at a pink and white cherry tree backed by a sky of azure blue murmured gently: 'What if two thousand have to die? It will be worth it'. To be fair to him I understood that he didn't just sit safely in New York thinking like that but travelled regularly to 'The Six Counties' to participate in the cause he believed in. But his words were chilling indeed, casting a dark shadow on a bright day.

Back in Dublin I continued to attend Ireland Fund meetings for some time under the chairmanship of Jim Sherwin and later Denis Whelan. In New York, on this second visit, a party was given for us by the staff of the Irish Consulate where Michael Lillis and Gearóid O'Cléirigh (a nephew of Mother Hogan's!) were endeavouring to make an outreach to those of Irish extraction in their catchment area who would previously have felt the need to examine their consciences if they darkened the doors of official Ireland, who were hugely in support of the hunger-strikers in Long Kesh, and who were not overjoyed to hear the views of 'The Cruiser' and of other government ministers on their visits to the United States. In Boston, Carmel Heaney's Consulate had recently been temporarily occupied by protesters and pickets were mounted there not infrequently. Now the New York Consulate was making a very special outreach and we, from Glencree, received advanced briefing that, if possible, we were to come in our jeans and not lay on any pearls or silks but just to tell our story like it really was. No doubt too, they privately hoped that I might not feel the need to say too much about my O'Higgins pedigree but, strangely enough, whenever I have been in discussions with actual Sinn Féin representatives (as well as those previously mentioned I have met Daithí O'Connaill, Seán MacStiophán, Pat Doherty, Mitchel McLoughlin, and others, and I have had letters and birthday greetings from Lucillita Breathnach and from Gerry Adams) I have experienced an odd sort of personal empathy rather than the contrary, because bereavements are always bereavements no matter what, and Republican tears and Free State tears taste much the same.

At any rate, the party that night seemed to go well and our hosts expressed considerable pleasure at the number and nature of those who attended. Over and over again, people I met said to me: 'That's the first time I ever heard anything about reconciliation coming out of Ireland. I have always believed that we must continue the struggle till the British go'. And some even said: 'Tell us more'.

More or less at the last minute before our departure from Dublin, Eleanor Wicklow (who, as Eleanor Butler, had been a Labour Senator before her marriage) had managed to get hold of the recent policy document of the Irish Congress of Trade Unions and had pressed it into my hand saying it might come in useful in America. 'Peace Jobs and Progress' were ICTU's priorities and the New York Consulate who had not yet seen the document grabbed it. Michael Lillis stayed up all night, I think, photocopying it, before ushering me onto a plane for Washington the next morning where he had made an appointment for me to meet one of the Vice-Presidents of A.F.L./C.I.O. (a major grouping of allied American trade unions) in order to discuss it. If only I were someone who actually knew something about Trade Unions, I thought, as I tried to study the paper on the shuttle to Washington where I pressed some hastily stapled photocopies of 'Peace and Jobs' into the hand of a rather lofty Swede. 'But ICTU is no longer affiliated to us so why should we pay attention?' he enquired. 'Because Michael Lillis says so', I felt like replying, but I hope I managed to say something more appropriate and at least he promised to include the document in his vast library where, he said, there were only two or three other publications from Ireland.

Following this trail of the American Unions and Noraid, I also called upon the Headquarters of the Longshoremen and of the Transport and General Workers, urging that their members contribute to reconciliation in Ireland rather than to the armed struggle. (In the case of some unions a percentage of the pay-packet was taken at source, I was told, to help the 'reunification' of Ireland). When gazing at that Taj Mahal of the Headquarters of American Trade Unionism in Washington, or in similar experiences, I would sometimes wonder how in heaven I had got there and heartily wish that someone more qualified were in my place. But I would have done a lot for Michael who, with Jane, made a deep impression on me and who subsequently from Government Buildings or from Iveagh House would occasionally tug at my sleeve to see if I could help out in other small ways. As for his later stint in Maryfield, following on the Anglo-Irish Agreement, I cannot imagine what life was like for those first incumbents but later I met some Unionists from that area with whom he had somehow managed to make friends and who had thought enough of him to travel south to celebrate with him his retirement from that position.

I have headed a previous chapter with Pearse's lines: 'Since the wise men have not spoken I speak that am only a fool' which were never far from me during this period of my life. At a meeting with Ian Paisley in Stormont they would have been in my mind but at least my clearheaded son, Eoin (also a member of Glencree) and Frank Purcell were there as well. Dr. Paisley swept us up in a personal welcome and the first thing that struck me was his enormous size and then his sea-green eyes. The day was that following the murders of the Miami Showband members and I remember being keen that Frank's Australian tones would be used to the taximen and in the streets of Belfast rather than our Dublin ones. Dr. Paisley was apparently in great humour that we had come to see him and was most cordial about his Catholic constituents and even about us in the South. The only problem was the IRA, he said. Prior to their campaign everyone had got on splendidly together, he maintained; Catholics would always milk the Protestant cows on the twelfth of July and Protestants would milk Catholic cows on the fifteenth of August. Moreover, the instruments that were used in the various marching bands were often lent from one group to the other – the titles on the drums being painted to suit whichever band was playing that day. I regretted that he had indicated at a very early stage to Peter Robinson that he should leave us; he was saying such agreeable things I would have wished to hear him saying them in the presence of one or two of his colleagues – something I stressed in my subsequent letter of thanks. With this letter I also sent him a copy of Terence de Vere White's biography of my father – a book which he later held aloft and quoted from in the House of Commons, I heard. Probably it was from the 'Do - we - think - they - [the Unionists]- will - come - hopping - across - the Border - like - fleas?' speech which many Unionists have cited approvingly to me as showing appropriate realism.

The period of the H-Block Hunger Strikes was the worst that I can remember in Dublin, as swarms of angry people descended upon the city in buses to join in rallies of protest, a number going on the rampage afterwards. Occasionally, I would make myself go down-town to listen to a speaker although Dublin 4 (an attitude of mind rather than a postal district) managed to remain detached. One Sunday afternoon I attended an overflow meeting in the Round Room of the Mansion House which was called in support of the Five Demands of Republican hunger-strikers. The meeting was chaired by Father Piaras O'Dubhghaill, O.F.M. Cap., and in due course I was called to the stage to make my contribution. (Once more the fool – but people's lives are worth a bit of foolishness, I thought). I said I could support four of the five demands and so, I imagined, would a lot of other people like me and was there a chance the fifth could be dropped? This was to do with loss of remission as a result of their protests. There may well have been serious issues involved in these demands but I could never think that their refusal – (the others were about prison uniform, freedom of association, prison work and receipt of one parcel per week) was worth the life of the Westminster M.P. Bobby Sands, much less nine other lives. I was followed immediately by a scathing young man with a very black beard who promptly rubbished my suggestion – a young man whose name, Gerry Adams, I hadn't heard before. Subsequently, Father O'Dubhghaill sent me a hand-written letter of apology saying that he should not have allowed that speaker to contravene Standing Orders as he had done by referring to the remarks of a previous speaker.

I felt very solitary in that gathering and was indeed grateful to Ulick O'Connor for saying kind things in my defence (come to think of it, *he* must have been in breach of Standing Orders also), and courageous things about my father as well. At my retirement from the Presidency of Glencree a few years ago, I received a card of warm wishes which was signed by Gerry Adams. Since I have never met him, I wonder whether this was in recognition of my attempt to express my grief that day about those young men on hunger strike who would soon be dead.

'The Lord be merciful to Kevin O'Higgins', said an elderly Republican removing his cap and making the Sign of the Cross when I told him, some years ago, who I was. Wearing his Easter lily, he had just made an impassioned speech in favour of the armed struggle outside a village church in the West of Ireland, after which I got a rush to the head and felt called upon to speak to him about my father's forgiveness for his assassins. Now, here he was extending the same forgiveness to me and to my father. There have been brief moments when I have felt that the whole situation is *not* insoluble, that somehow with one bound we *COULD* all be free, but then again that is probably the thought of a fool awaiting the wise people's speaking.

It was towards the beginning of the end of the fame of the Peace People that I first made real contact with Unionist East Belfast and with a number of women who earlier had entertained high hopes for the success of that movement. Initially, these Protestant women had joined in complete solidarity with Mairéad Corrigan and Betty Williams and their followers and it was they and their neighbours who had welcomed women from Catholic areas with open arms and stood shoulder to shoulder beside them in Ormeau Park – the first breakthrough. But by the time I met them a severe and ongoing problem had developed; their leaders had been supplanted, they said, and now only Catholics were visible on the platforms at the focal point of the weekly Marches. Apart from bruised feelings, there was a very serious side to this situation because, they said, while the Loyalist paramilitaries in their area *had* decided to put their operations on hold when they saw women from both communities joining together and getting such huge support, and had stood at the Rallies, hands in pockets, awaiting further developments, now, since they could see none of their own in the lead anymore, they were reaching once again for their weapons.

With hindsight, of course, I blame myself for being faint-hearted in the face of such dilemmas. Why was I satisfied to make only indirect, 'tactful' approaches to the Nobel prize-winners instead of insisting on talking with them face to face? Some time previously, as a guest of the Irish Association, I had shared a platform with Betty where Ciaran McKeown had also joined her. Couldn't I have followed up on that and asked them whether they realised the extent of the ferment among their previous colleagues in East Belfast? I suppose I didn't do it for the same reason that recently I did not take up an invitation to speak with the Garvaghy Road Residents in Portadown – because it is seldom that a blow-in from outside a situation has any credibility, and usually that's understandable. Could anyone from outside have made it clear to Ciaran McKeown that in fact this was a Women's Movement and one strictly based on non-violence *and on nothing else*? Women on both sides of the divide had shared a determination about one thing and one thing only – no more killing on *our* street – and they were prepared to be courageous enough to rattle their bin-lids and sound out that message in unison. They were agreed right across the province and in vast numbers on that – and they were agreed *on nothing else*. Not on ecumenism; many who had made friends while travelling together to the weekly Marches would still oppose marriages between their children. And certainly not on politics. They simply were a powerful voice for women across the divide, warning gunmen to keep out of their areas and denying them safe houses, and they should have been let get on with that enormous task.

I'm not saying that Betty, Mairéad and Ciaran didn't themselves have the talent, courage and commitment to do much more than that – on the contrary. But what they did not have was the *AGREEMENT* of those who walked with them for anything more than that. And, moreover, I have never ceased to wonder why three Catholics thought that alone, or with only very low-key Protestant presence in leadership at a later stage, they could successfully lead a Peace Movement in Northern Ireland. (It is not so much the wrongdoing of the wicked but the blindness of the good that can cause despair, at times!)

The blighting of women's hopes in East Belfast at that time was a calamity causing individual and group disintegration. I listened to endless painful stories and accusations – a penitential service – but I believed it had to be done in case there was any hope of reviving the trust that had originally given birth to the Peace People. And I was never sorry that I spent time with East Belfast Community Council members, whose friendship and hospitality became a very important part of my life; I am only sorry that I never came near to bridging that disastrous divide.

On the whole, I find women's meetings interesting and realistic and I warm to the sense of sisterhood that usually surfaces before long, no matter what the reason for the gathering. I think, for instance, of an ad hoc group of Northern and Southern women coming together at Glencree to discuss the conflict in the North. From opposite sides of the divide, and with strongly differing political opinions gained from active political involvement in their respective communities, they will almost certainly reach a degree of rapport before long because, too often, many share the same sorrows – alcoholism in the family, parental abuse in their childhood, desertion by a husband, rejection by a parent, depressions, unemployment, loss of a child, batterings, rape.

Much of this will get shared in a confidential atmosphere skilfully facilitated so that by the time they get round to discussing political problems they at least recognise and empathise with something of their opponents' background. And women's groups in the field of ecumenics, such as those which promote the Women's World Day of Prayer, for example, usually develop a strong internal bonding which transcends boundaries of organised religion without diminishing loyalty to their particular Church.

I wonder whether Mary Robinson fully realised the depth of response she would arouse with her one small phrase – 'Mná na hEireann'? – Did we know ourselves what it would mean to us to be quite suddenly understood, to be of real value and to inhale the oxygen of equality with those three little words?

CHAPTER TEN

'And Jesus said
"If you had but known the things that make for peace ..."'

After a spirited start the Glencree Centre, while it wasn't yet fulfilling a Yeatsian prophecy of not being able to hold, was beginning to experience a taste of things falling apart. Pressure as to whether it was or was not a Christian Centre became severe, so that the recitation of the 'Our Father' together became problematical and internal dissension about the appointment of Frank Purcell as Education Director, given the state of his dispute with the Society of St. Columban which had now been appealed to Rome, caused an amount of pain. At a later stage the Columbans themselves took hold of their difficulties, and considered setting up a reconciliation procedure with Frank. But there seems to have been a reluctance on the part of some or all of the former members to participate and so nothing came of it. At Glencree, the more conservative and possibly more faithful Catholics were, not surprisingly, unable to see that far ahead and they opted for caution about his appointment as our Education Director, preventing it unfortunately, by means which proved sadly divisive.

For me a number of things were clear.

While the motives of no human beings are entirely pure, Frank had honestly believed that he must pursue his insistence on human rights and due process for some of the novices within his Society, if he was to remain a member of its five-man Council (as he then was). They had a right to private correspondence, and if ordination was to be withheld, there must be frank disclosure about the reasons, he maintained. And, he also took quite literally that teaching of the Gospel where we are told not to come offering our gifts at the altar unless we are first reconciled to our brothers and sisters. So he believed a reconciliation must take place before he again celebrated Mass. His personal prayerfulness and his general handling of his critics as well as his good humour, generosity of spirit and fair-mindedness impressed me very much and I trusted his integrity. I believed that since he had done so much for us (we could never have made the start we did if he had not organised us, living in a basement flat of an otherwise deserted house in Camden Street on our wage of £30 per week); it was up to us to dialogue with the Columbans on his behalf in order, with considerable regret, to facilitate his return to them. This is not the place to chronicle the ins and outs of that struggle because I am party only to one side of the story, but to me it seemed lamentable that, only at a much later stage, did the Society of St. Columban come to understand what Frank had been trying to do for them in the area of human rights and due process. But happily today's leadership of that Society has offered warm hospitality to Frank and his wife on their forthcoming visit to Ireland.

Later, I believed that, as far as Glencree's difficulties arising out of the whole Frank Purcell problem were concerned, these must now be put behind us completely but that, without rehearsing the particular details of the episode which had caused the distrust among ourselves, we would need to work out for the future a method of due process so that we might be able to offer to others something which we had learned from our own experience of internal division. I have always been distinctly queasy about urging other people to become reconciled without being willing to engage in such a painful process oneself. Perhaps an extension of this problem is my malaise nowadays when, as frequently happens, congregations are asked to pray for peace in Ireland. While certainly it is true that every liturgy begins with a general acknowledgement of our own sinfulness and a prayer for forgiveness, there is something about praying for 'peace in the North' or 'peace in the north-eastern corner of our island' that bothers me, so that I have become less and less willing to ask the Lord graciously to hear us. Instead, I want to say to him: 'I'm not sure if we are fully ready to pray for peace. We have our own way of looking at things. Many of us believe that the whole island belongs to us (which is why even in this prayer we cannot use the name

'Northern Ireland') and have not a lot of time for the problem this poses for our brothers and sisters who prefer union with Britain. We may journey on pilgrimages and praise you in foreign places but we don't often travel across the Border to find how both communities there view us. Is it right to expect you to deliver peace unless we realise that we ourselves are part of the problem?'

But it's so easy to be convinced about the correctness of one's own point of view and it's so much more difficult to persuade others of its merit! Meantime, the Columbans had preferred to manage without much dialogue with us and a rather battered Frank had retired to Australia to grow wines for a time, while Glencree soldiered on trying to pick up the pieces and to revive our earlier momentum. For a while I became its Organising Secretary myself, though I doubt if organising has ever been my forte. When eventually the office was moved from Harcourt Street to Belgrave Square, other extensions of our efforts developed around the same time: the use of a house in Ballysillan in Belfast, generously lent to us by Rev. Tim Kinahan, and the gift of a farm beside the Centre at Glencree – kindly donated by Desmond and Dorothea Good. By then George Ferguson had taken the position of Organising Secretary and the house in Belgrave Square was often used to accommodate overnight stays of people from the North, so everything seemed to hum.

Looking back on those years, however, I feel we over-reached ourselves, taking on too many new responsibilities at the same time, but it can be difficult to say 'no' to grants and loans and to refuse generous offers of property. I was never on the financial side of things and no doubt was overawed by our Development Committee which for some time contained some very big names but I do feel guilty about not keeping more contact with, for example, the Belfast house and similar regrets plague me. Moreover, the lack of an agreed and structured form of due process among ourselves continued to haunt me so that, for some years, I withdrew, reconnecting, as promised, when a Membership Committee undertook to monitor and mediate internal disputes for the future. Eventually, however, I was to lose confidence again and, with a deep sense of bereavement, to take my leave of that group who, before many more years had passed, had to put up the shutters on their undertakings and suspend operations in 1989.

Heartbreak indeed.

What does it matter by which road you walk
to Portadown? You still are you
and nothing in the pavements of Garvaghy
will make you different. The air
is no more healthy there
and you are no more free
because you march in front of Catholics,
wearing your sashes, banging your drums
to honour your tradition
and conserve your culture.
Say, is it likely those who perished at the Somme
would understand the deaths of three young children
as hallowing their memory?
What does it matter now how you return
to your home town?

FOR THE FREEDOM FIGHTERS

How is it possible to deal out death
while spiders weave their jewelled miracles
through mists of morning heather
wrapping the moors in filigree adornment,
while song-birds fling their 'Alleluias'
to the skies and butterflies besiege the buddleias
in confident renewal?

How is it possible to plan for death
while small boats tumble on a buoyant lake
and cuckoos call from rural fastnesses
where honeysuckles clamber through the hedgerows?
How plan to kill where blackberries
redden the searching fingers with sweet juices,
not blood sacrifice?

How execute life's end while faithfully
dark winters germinate their secret plans
preparing resurrection? How share
in spring's glad seminars while choking out
the life-breath of another — claiming
that this will foster union?
Name your campaign
as hatred or revenge, but leave aside
your fallacy of fusion!

CHAPTER ELEVEN

Hung from every lamp-post.

1977 was a startling year. The previous autumn Eoin and I had bought and moved into the house on Cross Avenue, Booterstown, where my father had died and from which I had been born five months prior to his death. 'Dunamase' had been renamed more than once in the meantime but we went back to the name of the Laoighis fortress after which my parents had named it. Although I had only spent my very early months there, it held powerful resonances for me and, growing up at a distance, it always seemed to me to contain a part of myself with which I needed to re-connect. When I was young, a class-mate then inhabiting it invited me once to her party but I had had to concentrate so hard in order not to fall off her pony that I retained no memories of the house itself! By 1976 most of our family were attending lectures in Belfield and so 'Dunamase' was ideal from their point of view. Likewise, while the lease on White Lodge had run out, 'Dunamase' proved very accommodating for their friends and also for the many meetings which were convened there in the run-up to the general election of 1977 and for other groupings.

What happened about the election took us all by surprise, I think. *The Irish Times* had been running a series of articles concerning the brutality of the so-called Garda 'Heavy Gang'. This was a subject that hit me on two fronts: firstly as a peace-worker who believed in the even-handed administration of justice and the necessity for accountability and, secondly, because my father had been immensely proud of the Guards and he would have been angered and saddened to see them transgressing in such ways. So one thing led to another until I heard myself saying something like: 'I've a good mind to run as an independent candidate in the election myself if no-one else will highlight this disaster'. To this came an immediate and earnest response from Eoin Junior: 'If you do, I'll be your agent'. Shock, horror, but before long we were 'on' and approximately one hundred canvassers had joined us in 'Dunamase' to spread the message that, if you were talking about peace, you were talking of human rights and accountability in the administration of justice.

Whether they each agreed exactly with what I was saying or with each other I'm not sure, but each slaved to win me a seat in Dun Laoghaire for reasons that seemed good to them and they were so loyal that, when eventually their candidate was eliminated, it wasn't only women who shed tears. I am proud to look now on one or two leading lawyers and human rights activists who, when younger, joined that campaign and I am glad that it was mounted – although it was painful to challenge the Taoiseach, Liam Cosgrave, in his own constituency, especially since my father and his had been close colleagues.

A very important support group at that time was the Women's Political Association. Who would not be energised by people such as Gemma Hussey, Hilary Pratt, Mavis Arnold and their associates? All in all, we gave it our best shot and, had there been five seats then as now, we would have made it. As it was, Martin O'Donoghue took what Auntie Mo had come to regard as 'Una's seat' and all that remained to be done was to take down the posters.

But not quite all. As a result of raising my head above the parapet on the subject of human rights, I began to be looked for and to join various other projects – the Committee of the Irish Council for Civil Liberties (ICCL) – under the chairmanship of Kader Asmal – was one, and, as already mentioned, membership of Seán MacBride's Commission of Enquiry into the Penal System initiated by Joe Costello of the Prisoner's Rights Organisation was another.

Somewhere in those years I also served time with Co-operation North. Dr. Brendan O'Regan had invited representatives of some voluntary groups into the project to help get it going, as well as heavy-weights such as bankers and business people. I was there on behalf of Glencree with Brigid Wilkinson from the Irish Association and Kate O'Callaghan from Limerick and Sheila Goldberg from Cork. Brigid was also a mate in the ICCL and in many other ventures; a woman of charm, humour and considerable judgement. Noticing how deftly captains of industry handle each other and deal with obstacles that come their way can be revealing. Do women have quite the same opportunities to socialise in clubs and smooth things over prior to meetings, I wondered? No doubt by now they do.

Another result of my election campaign was my convening and chairing an ad-hoc cross-party group composed of the women politicians of Dun Laoghaire constituency to see what, if anything, could be done about the travelling people in that area. The welfare of travellers was a subject which concerned many members of peace groups. After his time in Glencree, Father Shaun Curran gave his services to developing a school for travelling boys while Victor Bewley's support for travellers was in line with the amazing witness of the Society of Friends. Now an all-party group of women politicians in Dun Laoghaire came together at 'Dunamase' to enquire into the situation of travelling-people in that constituency and to receive briefings from one or two very committed officials of Dublin Corporation and County Council who demonstrated real concern and commitment to the subject. Subsequently, in the company of Ethna Nolan, a well-known activist on behalf of travellers, I made representations to Dublin County Council at one or two formal sittings. I was sorry when eventually this group had to admit that there was nothing more we could usefully do at that stage because it had seemed to me that an all-party group of concerned politicians was accorded substantial responses from officialdom.

After that election campaign also I considered joining the Labour Party and had an interview with Frank Cluskey in the party rooms in Leinster House. But I heard nothing further from him on that score; no doubt there were delicacies in Dun Laoghaire to be considered.

Earlier in the 1970s I had been invited to join the Committee of the Irish Association – a group in which I have experienced many kindnesses. As soon as names are listed some will invariably be omitted but friends like Donal and Eileen Barrington, Ruairí and Maire Brugha, Doreen Freer, Brian

Garrett, Hugh Monro, Ann Murphy, Orla Ruttledge, John McBratney, Declan White, would never have come my way except for the Irish Association. Subsequent to my period of Presidency of the Association, Father Enda McDonagh presided over it in such a way that he even managed to put what was a fairly impoverished organisation into financial stability. Around that time also, Barbara Sweetman Fitzgerald became its Director after which everything was taken care of.

The conference which remains most in my mind was that held in Dun Laoghaire in 1984 – the same weekend that the Conservative Conference in Brighton was bombed by the IRA. The reality of that atrocity was vividly brought home to us because some of our speakers and guests would otherwise have been in Brighton and were anxiously hanging on to telephones in the Royal Marine Hotel to get news of friends and colleagues caught up in the blast.

Security at our conference was so tight that when, at lunchtime on the Saturday, the British Ambassador, Sir Alan Goodison, asked me to take a walk with him down the pier (it was a glorious day) we were accompanied by at least a dozen Gardaí. The evening before there had been a hasty phone call from Iveagh House after the news from Brighton: 'The bad news is that the Minister (Peter Barry) will not be giving the keynote address to your meeting tonight as arranged; the good news is that the Taoiseach (Garret FitzGerald) will be coming instead to make a statement'. This was not, in fact, good news for many of our Unionist members who had travelled south in order to pepper Peter Barry with questions and give him a taste of how they felt about his green nationalism. Instead, a white-faced Taoiseach accompanied by a team of handlers and a posse of journalists swept in to read a terse statement before the bright lights and was swept away again before anybody got a chance to say anything to him. But it is not, of course, for the voluntary sector to reason why and in the main we were glad to be of service as we gathered ourselves together again in the dimness of the normal lighting.

Another memorable meeting of the Irish Association was held in the City Hall, Belfast, which was hosted by a DUP Lord Mayor, Nigel Dodds at which the Secretary-General of the

Commonwealth, Sir Shridath (Sonny) Ramphal, was the guest speaker. It was good to see the Mayor sharing a platform with our Vice-President, Father Enda McDonagh from Maynooth, and I greatly enjoyed the address of the Secretary-General although I did wonder if it had not been intended for a southern audience, since he stressed strongly all that the Irish delegation had done in the early part of this century to help what was then the British Commonwealth develop its present egalitarian reality, and quoted a quip (in fact, my father's) about how the bacon which General Smuts had claimed to bring home to South Africa was actually 'Irish bacon'.

Someone who had little difficulty with that claim, it subsequently emerged, was the late Peadar O'Donnell. In the early 1980s, after the funeral in the Mater Hospital of Doctor Kevin Malley, brother of Ernie O'Malley (no relation of Eoin's), I introduced myself to O'Donnell since he was alone at the Mass and was, by that time, blind. 'The men who killed your father', he assured me:

> did a bad day's work for Ireland. We (the IRA) had an informant giving us daily reports on the Imperial Conference of 1926 for £1,000 (one thousand pounds) per day and we could find no fault with what O'Higgins and his colleagues were doing for Ireland. He should have been let get on with his work. But then ... we Irish never could pull together the way the British can ...

The evening of Sir Sonny Ramphal's visit to Belfast ended with a dinner at Hillsborough Castle, where he further impressed us, speaking of his native Guyana with almost Irish intonations. Not so impressive, however, was the speech of the hosting British Minister, I'm afraid, who seemed rather like a comic legacy from a previous century – a far cry from Chris Patten and Nicholas Scott whose services in the Northern Ireland Office impressed me considerably.

Other friends I made through the Irish Association were the McGimpsey brothers who stayed at 'Dunamase' when presenting their case to the Forum for a New Ireland. As Brian Garrett, who succeeded me as President, used to say, there was a touch of old lace about the Association in our day but now, largely due to Barbara Sweetman Fitzgerald, it has attained a much higher profile. In 1998 it celebrated its sixtieth year – no mean feat for a north-south voluntary group that has managed to survive through many years of tension and near despair.

It was with Glencree Part II, under the leadership of Colin Murphy, that I eventually became reconnected. Colin (whom I had not known previously) had been a member of the last Council of Glencree which had decided on its closure and he had remained determined to do everything he could to bring about its revival. This he compared to taking a patient into intensive care and working for their resuscitation. When after some years he succeeded in keeping a flicker of life alive in his patient to the point where he believed he was ready for a re-launch, all the old guard were again contacted – including myself. I wavered and dithered as to whether or not to become re-involved but when I considered all the effort that had gone into its original establishment, the sacrifices that had been made by so many people at all levels, I felt I had little option. So I signed on once again and enjoyed some more years before retiring in 1997 from its Presidency. It is great to see the old place vibrating once more with many valuable political workshops under the guidance of Geoffrey Corry (another of the old guard), while Ian White has been a most committed and dynamic Director. I wish there were many more places like it where people are encouraged to listen and to learn from each other how the other half lives and where young people get an opportunity to examine and evaluate their own prejudices. As I write, a whole new development is being undertaken in the old barracks – a project in which I find myself once more involved and it is great, too, to see the new wing designed by Eleanor Wicklow being made so useful. In our early days we had learned to see Peace as imagined not so much in paintings but in mosaics – a picture formed of thousands of individual pieces, *every one of which is needed* if the harmony is to prevail. I like that concept very much.

For myself I would have much preferred if Glencree could have held on to shared prayer and had become again an interdenominational Christian community – something Colin, as a Corrymeela member, would also have wanted. But that did not prove to be the consensus when the project was being re-launched. Instead, there is a commitment to pluralism – pluralism in the true sense that any group broadly in keeping with the aims and objectives of the organisation is as welcome to use the facilities there as any other. So if prayer-groups wish to avail of it they are welcome and indeed the many worshippers (known as 'The Little Ones') who visit the church at Glencree on a regular basis often visit the Centre too as welcome guests.

For me the whole experience has been a learning one, although I sometimes have pangs when I try to work out whether my family was neglected in the course of all this. 'Finbarr, would you ever put the spuds on', or, if he sounded sufficiently cheerful, 'would you be on for making a cake?' I would request over the phone, while Iseult would arrive up to Harcourt Street from Loreto, Stephen's Green, and resignedly begin her homework, waiting for me to get away from the office. Eoin Jr., as I have said, was a founder member of Glencree while Chris later was employed by the group for a while as its Development Officer. Whenever I felt guilty about the family and about what Eoin might have been deprived of because of all this extra-mural activity on my part, I would remind myself of what it had felt like to grow up fatherless and I believed that what we were doing in our small way was necessary if other children's fathers were to have more of a chance. Moreover, I hoped that the Father of us all would make up the deficit.

One of my last tasks in the active service of Glencree was in 1995 to lead a joint Submission to the Forum for Peace and Reconciliation, then sitting in Dublin Castle, which we made together with the Corrymeela Community. This, unfortunately, involved exact timekeeping and, since we had had no opportunity to rehearse together with the Corrymeela team, I was a bit on edge, which, no doubt, is why I passed a note to a Northern member on the very dot of her allotted time asking her to wind up as soon as possible. Immediately she did just that, stopping almost in mid-sentence with some surprise and hurt. Not so another friend, the one who subsequently asked in astonishment: 'Did I really take THAT long?' Three notes from me and a personal messenger from the Forum's Chair, Judge Catherine McGuinness, had failed to achieve the desired effect. 'Did you take that long?' said another colleague. 'Sure they were almost having to cut the floorboards from under you'. I had some regrets about agreeing to handle our timing on that day!

Some years ago also I used to chair an occasional meeting in Dublin for the Peace Institute whose headquarters are in Limerick University. These were arranged by Dorothy Cantrell, usually for visiting groups of Americans who wanted to know more about the Northern Ireland situation. I soon was impressed by a polite young man who sometimes spoke for the Unionist position and I have since watched his swift rise to the front ranks of his Party with some awe. Jeffrey Donaldson, now Deputy Grand Master of the Orange Order, not only handled his audiences well (the views of many of those Americans were distinctly green in hue) but even managed to hit it off with the local Fianna Fáil deputy, Councillor Tom Stafford, since then Dublin's Lord Mayor.

GOOD FRIDAY 1998

At three o'clock
with well-directed blows
the burly carpenter
hammered the Cathedral cross
into its socket,
shocking Carlow's hushed attendance
with the starkness of Friday's story
presented then artistically on screen
by young and very reverent people.
By five o'clock
there was no news as yet
of signatures in Stormont
and the sound of the hammered blows
re-echoed in my being.

But at 6 pm
I lit our Easter candle
holding in flame together
the dead and the creative living
now come to their agreement,
and I drank the celebratory wine
for, on this very best of days,
we all had been remembered.

CHAPTER TWELVE

' ... and forgive us our trespasses as we forgive those who
trespass against us ...'

The concept of forgiveness as an ingredient of politics in
any recognisable way was first put to me by Professor Haddon
Willmer of the Department of Theology in Leeds University
when he spoke at Glencree, something he subsequently
elaborated on in an article in *The Furrow* magazine in April
1979 (see appendix). The idea that forgiveness was actually a
factor without which ordinary politics could not work – albeit
an unacknowledged factor – was fascinating. Before long a
study-group was set up in England dealing with The Politics
of Forgiveness with Brian Frost, author of *The Politics of Peace*
and biographer of Lord Soper, as its executive. (Brian has also
produced a small book called *Women and Forgiveness* in which
he has included some ideas that I had developed along the
way). I became an out-of-town member of this group and once
had the honour of addressing a congregation at the Methodist
Central Mission in London at the invitation of the Rev. Leslie
Griffith and of Brian.

An Inter-Church Group on Faith and Politics, otherwise
known as the 'Faith and Politics' group, however, is an all-*Irish*
body meeting alternately north and south of the border and
producing documents on testing subjects of the day. Among
its publications are: 'Breaking Down the Enmity' in 1985;
'Understanding the Signs of the Times' (1986); 'Towards an
Island that Works' (1987); 'Towards Peace and Stability – A
Critical Assessment of the Anglo-Irish Agreement' (1988);
'Remembering our Past: 1690–1916' (1991); 'Burying our Dead
– Political Funerals' (1992); 'Liberty to the Captives?' (1995);
'Forgive us our Trespasses' (1996); 'Doing Unto Others' (1997);
'New Pathways' (1997), 'Remembering and Forgetting' (1998)
and most recently 'Transitions' (2001). Taking part in its
meetings means an early start for those at the other end of the

railway line, but I always enjoyed the meetings and they also kept me in contact with Corrymeela and with some of its leaders.

Some years previously, when Rev. Ray Davey, founder of the Corrymeela Community, was invited to give one of the celebrated Sunday evening talks at Great St. Mary's in Cambridge, he did me the honour to ask me to be his partner and to present a southern perspective on 'the troubles'. Our host was the Rev. Michael Mayne, formerly of the BBC and subsequently Chaplain to the Speaker of the House of Commons. In Great St. Mary's there are two pulpits, one on either side of the church – which are reached by quite a long flight of stairs – or so it seemed to me. I mention them because that morning when bending over to put the stopper in the bath in the Mayne's hospitable home I ricked my back, something which was then a new experience. The rest of the household had gone to Church – I was to go to mine later – and I was alone in the house wondering if I would ever be able to straighten up again. Most of the day was spent amid aspirins and hot-water bottles and by evening Ray and I were able to process gingerly down the long aisle and I made it to 'my' pulpit. Perhaps it was as well that the physical side of things preoccupied me so that I had little time left in which to be nervous. I had never spoken in a church. The Maynes couldn't have been kinder and, thanks to Michael, I had an interview next day with the BBC World Service on my way through London (something which Father John Feighery heard in Peru at 4.00 am when he turned on his radio for a time check).

Because of having to take my back very cautiously, I saw nothing else of Cambridge but, in the days of my youth, I had stayed in one of the Oxford Colleges for a week, or rather in the home of its President, whose son had invited me to be his partner for some of the famous Commem. Balls of that era. This invitation had raised my stock greatly amongst the neighbours at the Baily at the time and I was straightaway presented with a copy of 'Zuleika Dobson' in order to get in the mood for celebrations by one still nostalgic for his days of dancing until dawn, followed by champagne breakfasts and punting on the river. So I carefully folded my grey and white striped taffeta garden-party dress with its big bell-sleeves and whatever ball-gowns I could muster for the week's festivities. 'Oh, do come and listen to her', a group of young men urged each other when I attended the first Reception. 'She has got the most delicious brogue!' That, although I had been far from trying out my Pegeen Mike routine or my Mollser act from 'Plough and the Stars'!

I remember – who could forget? – the chiselled countenance of Edith Sitwell in her turbaned hat, there with her brothers to receive an honorary degree. I remember how we anxiously kept refreshing the flowers in their silver vases in the President's drawing room all week so as to be ready to receive General McArthur who might drop in at any minute after he had called upon his former batman, then living in the gate lodge. (When the famous General finally did come to the President's residence everybody was out except my hostess who happened to be in her wellingtons feeding the hens). At the Ball given by 'our' College, I saw Princess Margaret among the guests dancing to the music of the numerous bands which, in turn, kept the show on the road until the dawn broke. In those days (as in May week in Cambridge) students held no organised dances or parties during the rest of the academic year, saving up their energies for one magic week during which they slept not at all, I think.

In East Hendred in Oxfordshire, many years after my dancing days were over, I spoke in the Catholic church there about peace in Ireland and about forgiveness. This was at the invitation of the Parish Priest, Father Tony ffrench-Mullen, an old friend. 'We do not take in *The Tablet*', said one of his parishioners to me – I imagine because it was considered too radical. Yet this lady, from the Manor House, where a very elderly and old-style chaplain resided (the family traces a relationship to St. Thomas More and their chapel contains some important relics of him) had, with her brother, also developed a staunch loyalty to Father Anthony (Tony), her parish priest – a man of very different style and outlook.

Tony ffrench-Mullen had been ordained from the Beda College in Rome, being a 'late vocation' (at the age of twenty-seven). The Beda, he would say, had only two rules – You must not knock out your pipe into the holy water font was one; I forget the second. But I know he maintained that the statue of the Blessed Virgin in its Chapel was miraculous because it was the only one in Italy that did not weep and when as a seminarian there, he sent me a first-class relic of my patron saint, Agnes; the card with it said: 'a chip off the old block'. Tony had been a bomber-pilot in the RAF and had been a prisoner of war in Germany for a number of years before helping to organise and take part in one of the great escapes. Between that and entering the Beda he wrote the libretto for a musical that was staged in London's West End; he was a man of many parts. Later he joined the Cistercian Community on Caldey Island and helped to develop its perfumery. Somehow, some way, by the end of his life he had appealed to people right across the spectrum, from this lady of the old school for whom *The Tablet* was too strong, to some pretty unorthodox people who also recognised a good man when they met one. Not that things had been easy for him along the way. I think the prison experience always haunted him, causing him to leave the enclosed atmosphere of Caldey Monastery after 17 years but at the time of his death his parishioners celebrated with parties for a week, because this is what he had instructed them to do. Going to heaven was something to party about, he insisted; everyone should don their best clothes and have a ball when he went! And so they did – the children one day, older people on another, parish groups on a third, and so it went on until the week was over. Friends travelled long distances to be part of the celebrations; volunteers in the parish (who must have taken the time out of their annual holidays) directed the streams of traffic, people opened their houses, the lady of the manor threw a huge party, while other gatherings were hosted in the school and in the nearby Anglican convent. Everybody was *en fête* together.

On the day of the funeral, Archbishop Derek Worlock gave the homily which at times was difficult to hear because of a summer storm raging outside. When one huge clap of thunder fairly shook the church and knocked over the bishop's glass of water, he threw an appealing glance heavenward: 'Alright, Tony, we know you are up there but just turn down the sound a bit, will you?' he pleaded.

Perhaps the reason why people related so much to this unusual priest was because he was willing to share himself with them; his house was the parish centre where meetings always took place and the key to which lots of people had. In his last illness he managed, somehow, to remain there with his people while they continued to come and go because he wanted them to learn not to fear death. Devoted friends took turns nursing him until finally he had his way and, through their tears, people rejoiced as they sang with the widely smiling West Indian guitarist who led us through the rain to his graveside: 'Alleluia, Alleluia, give thanks to the Risen Lord, Alleluia, Alleluia, sing praise to his name'. Another remarkable feature of that parish was its Primary School where one hundred children seemed able to co-exist in an atmosphere of great peace. Looking at them all playing together at break-time I saw no teachers in charge, yet there seemed to be no pushing or fighting, everybody seemed to be involved in some activity and no one seemed lonely or left out. When I commented on this to the Principal, he said he thought it was due to having no system of competition with each other – each pupil competed only with themselves. The aim was to improve on your own marks of last week, not to do better than your friends. So much of life is framed adversarially, he said, that it's no wonder we have the wars and conflicts that we endure. Moreover, he said, it was important to try really hard to discover some special strength of each pupil and encourage the others to appreciate it and to lean upon it, when appropriate. I suppose a short visit to a school doesn't tell a visitor everything but I certainly was struck by the happy atmosphere in that one when I called.

At home very formative experiences for me were the Theology Courses run by *The Furrow* magazine under its editor Father Ronan Drury. I had heard priests such as the Glencree member, Father Denis Greene, S.M., insist on the priesthood of the laity ('What are you?' he might ask a small boy before Sunday Mass in the church at Glencree, 'a priest, Father', would be the reply which would be rewarded with an approving pat on the head) – but it was another matter to learn at those *Furrow* courses that, not only were we all priests, but that we were 'doing theology' as we journeyed together in faith. Togetherness was emphasised also by the attendance of Garret FitzGerald whenever he had time – his wife, Joan, was generally able to stay longer – and by the British Ambassador, Sir Alan Goodison, a lay-reader in the Church of England. In fact, sometimes their two sets of Garda 'minders' would be stationed outside our deliberations. Inside, a cross-section of eager people – not all of us as distinguished as those I have mentioned – were finding encouragement, something valuable for us all but perhaps especially so for women. By now it almost causes me no surprise (*ALMOST* but not quite) to be invited to write 'homilies', or an article for a religious journal such as *The Furrow*, but in the 1980s I think the few women who were included in religious publications were mainly religious Sisters. But true to its name, *The Furrow* opened up new places for seeds to be sown. Let's hope we have not been heretical! At the same time *Doctrine and Life*, under the editorship of Father Austin Flannery, O.P., was also offering a welcome and he was always most approachable and warmly supportive.

In 1979, several months prior to the Pope's visit to Dublin, a number of us involved in peace groups and in similar undertakings became uneasy because no interdenominational religious event was being planned. Accordingly, a committee was formed which I was asked to chair and which came up with the idea that, on the night of the Holy Father's arrival, a Peace Vigil should be held in St. Patrick's Church of Ireland Cathedral. Once again, I was a fool on a wise one's errand and I never succeeded, try as I might, in establishing contact with the official committee which was arranging the Papal programme, although I had personal friends on it. The main momentum to honour the Pope in this ecumenical way was coming from Protestants. As a member of the Committee of Glenstal's Ecumenical Conference for several years, my impression was somewhat similar – most of the motivation to keep the Conference going, apart from the zeal of that community itself, was coming from Protestant rather than Catholic clergy. (A number of Catholic lay people were very supportive).

If our project was to take shape in St. Patrick's, we were faced with one enormous difficulty. Four sponsors were needed for the occasion and two distinguished Protestants had already lent their names, together with the Abbot of Glenstal. But before long it was clear that the latter could only leave his name if he was joined by a member of the Catholic hierarchy and the problem was that bishops were only to give their names to an event which appeared on the hierarchy's own official programme. Sadly, this catch 22 situation almost defeated us and I felt that we were very near the end of the line and would have to abandon the project until, faintly but firmly, the voice of the Bishop of Ossory, Dr. Peter Birch, came over a bad line: 'Ah sure they know I'm only an old fellow living far from the road and they'll forgive me, so put my name to it, by all means'. I don't know when I heard a more beautiful message more sweetly put.

On the night in question St. Patrick's was *en fête* – its bells and those of Christ Church practically breaking their hearts in welcome. The overflow congregation, led by President Hillery, several government ministers and members of the diplomatic corps, included Cardinal Willebrands, President of the Vatican Secretariat for Christian Unity. It even included an auxiliary bishop of Dublin, in the end of the day! In spite of wild rumours circulating in the press corps (Henry Kelly, who came with Conor Brady from *The Irish Times*, borrowed my car to dash off for a special photographer), it did not, however, include the Pope, although Rev. Ernest Gallagher, representing the Methodist Church at an earlier reception at the Nunciature, had promised to put him into his 'deux chevaux' if necessary and drive him down from the Cabra Road himself! Later a senior Garda officer told me that he had kept a (no doubt more suitable) car and outriders at the ready at the Nunciature during the hours of the St. Patrick's Vigil 'just in case ...' because it was, in his opinion, the single most significant thing the Pope could have done for peace during his whole Irish visit. The Gardaí must have been terribly stretched at that time but they seemed to manage admirably. In St. Patrick's that afternoon there had been a sudden scramble because while the eyes of Security were, of course, trained upon the Pope, it became clear that the President and a lot of other VIPs would be assembled in St. Patrick's that night so hastily hassocks had to be thumped and alcoves searched to make sure that all was well there too. Shortly before the service began I realised that we would need to unstack the extra folding-chairs which we had hired in case they were needed and which were piled high in the porch. So I asked a long-haired hippie-type young man who was standing near me with his hands in the pockets of his leather jerkin if he would be good enough to help me to get them opened. Without removing his hands from his pockets he said politely: 'I would indeed, Ma'am, except that I'm here to look after your guests'. 'Plain clothes' came then in many varieties. But there was a moment when Garda efficiency almost excluded 'the Starving of the World' from our prayers! A group of actors had prepared a section of the vigil in which, dressed in rags and crying and wailing, they were to enter the Cathedral portraying the suffering of the Third World. 'Shut the doors', a Garda urged hastily, 'it's a H-Block Demo'. (Sad old world?)

But before we dispersed that night our patron Bishop Birch came down from the Nunciature bringing a special greeting and blessing from the Pope for those assembled in the Cathedral in his honour. And speaking about the lesser-known famine which had taken place in Ireland exactly a century before, the Bishop said that if we wanted to find peace we would have to do what our ancestors had done at that time, pull ourselves up by our own bootstraps. I believed him then and I believe him now. It will not be sufficient for politicians to come together to carve out agreements – essential though such things may be; the rest of us must dedicate ourselves to bridge-building also wherever and however we can. Thankfully, Eoin's surgical skills were not needed during that papal visit, during which Archbishop Dermot Ryan had asked him to be close to the celebrated visitor all the time he was in the Dublin archdiocesan area with plasma and whatever else might be required in case of emergency. Dr. Ivo Drury, a well-known physician, was likewise in attendance, but neither of them actually ever got to meet the Pope, although their car had to tear after his wherever he went and they slept in the Nunciature close to him so as to be at the ready.

But I met the Holy Father myself the following year – something beyond my wildest expectations! It came about as the result of a very poignant meeting held at Corrymeela, arranged there by the Politics of Forgiveness group. 'There's got to be another way, there's got to be another way', moaned one young participant rocking in pain with his head in his hands, and indeed we were all greatly distressed by what we had experienced in the past decade. So when it was decided that one of the Protestant Unionists present should seek an audience with the Pope and I was asked to go along as well, I was delighted. Of course, I did not think that we would actually receive such a private audience but, after many months of negotiations through Belfast, there we were alone with him in the Papal study and he was scrutinising the two of us very keenly. With the assistance of a small group of consultants at home, I had produced a thirteen-page document mainly setting out my conviction that somehow Irishness and Catholicism must be separately identified and separately honoured and appealing to him to help us on that score in the cause of peace. My companion also submitted a paper to the Holy Father primarily highlighting 'the plight of the much maligned British Irish of Northern Ireland'. While I did not think that the Pope himself would have time to read such papers, I took courage early on in the interview and requested that he would ask someone close to him to read my paper and to relate to him its main thrust. He gave me a long searching look but said nothing in reply and continued the meeting as if he had not heard. We had twenty minutes with him – twenty minutes in which he conveyed a deep sense of LISTENING, so much so that I doubt I have met anyone else who seemed to listen so intently. Just as we were on our feet to leave and I was wondering WHAT to do with my portfolio he turned to me saying: 'Give me your paper; I will read it myself. You must keep in touch with me', he urged us both. 'How shall we know you receive our letters?' I had the nerve to enquire. 'Of course I will. My secretary is Irish', he replied. But only a few weeks later he was attacked in St. Peter's Square and letters that we sent subsequently were acknowledged by some polite Monsignor who assured us that the Holy Father was praying for us. My Protestant friend was deeply affected by the whole experience and we were greatly saddened by the murderous attack in the Piazza San Pietro.

Previous second or third-hand experiences I had with officialdom in Rome had been off-putting but this was something else! The small portress-sister at the Convent of the Trinita dei Monte, where we had been made welcome since I was an 'ancienne' of the Society of the Sacred Heart, had actually sounded as if she was wiping the floor with whoever she spoke to at the Vatican when enquiring why we had not heard from them about the precise last-minute timing for our visit. All she knew was that her Reverend Mother expected her to find out what were the details and nobody was going to stand in her way. It was a question of priorities and seemingly Reverend Mother came way ahead of Vatican bureaucracy.

'My son, you must never fall out with Rome', a young Englishman whom years earlier Eoin and I had met on holiday in Switzerland was warned. This was Father Paul Weir who some weeks previously had stood up in his parish church in Tunbridge Wells and said that there was a letter concerning the recent papal encyclical *Humanae Vitae* which he had been asked to read aloud but that he did not feel able to do so. So as a guest of the Swiss-Irish management of our hotel, he was then endeavouring to come to terms with the situation by vigorous walking in the nearby mountains. 'I will lift my eyes to the hills ...' While in Switzerland he was hoping also to consult with Professor Hans Küng but, when someone from Tubingen did come to see him, it was not Kung but a much older and more cautious individual who offered the above warning. I'm afraid it did not carry much weight with Paul, whose temperament had more to do with one of the theme songs of that day, 'I did it my way ... '. The loss of a talented and caring priest such as he seemed to me a tragedy. Later I was to meet many others who had come adrift because of that encyclical and for various other reasons, but this was an early experience and it hit us hard. I would love to have been able to talk with the Pope about all of this, about former members of religious orders, loosed into society hardly knowing what size shoes they wore, so much had everything been taken care of for them by their Bursar. 'Three square meals a day and no heavy lifting', one man described his way of life until he had found himself sharing a basement flat in the inner city with a kindly colleague while wondering where his next meal would come from. Did their former Superiors or communities keep in touch with them in a caring way, I wondered? Perhaps they did, but I never seemed to hear about it then. For me there is something heart-warming about a parish priest in County Galway who always includes in his Mass not just 'James, our bishop', but also 'Eamonn, our former bishop'. In a world fraught with painful divisions wouldn't it be compelling if Mother Church were always seen to be a loving mother to ALL her children no matter in what circumstances they find themselves? Mothers in the main are like that, aren't they, and Christ does not seem to have mentioned betrayal when he talked with his followers after his Resurrection.

In Rome too, I thought about a woman who had, with members of her support group, sought me out at the time of my election campaign. These were people all of whom maintained that their marriages had been unjustly annulled by the Church without their consent. Mary Robinson was acting as lawyer for this woman and, in due course, I put her in touch also with a canon lawyer who advised her to appeal to the Apostolic Signatura in Rome. To the best of my knowledge, she heard no more from there although unwisely she had sent some important original documentation in support of her case. But I may not know the full story. What I did know was quite enough to go on with and I hope that the more recent protests of Joseph Kennedy's Episcopalian wife will do good. On the face of it, anyway, it was difficult to grasp how my 'client' with four school-going children – two born during the period of the union and two others legally adopted by both parents during that time also – could be told that, in fact, she and her partner had never been married. By the time I met her she was in a state of agitated beleagueredness – which certainly didn't help her case – but it was hard to blame her, since she felt abandoned both by Church and State. Her partner was embarking on a second union which had been solemnised by the Church while the Director of Public Prosecution's office would handle no objections to it. After that experience (as I say I may not know the full story but there did appear to be serious questions to be answered) I have thought that, at the very least, a civil form of marriage separate and distinct from the church ceremony, as in many other countries, would be a better arrangement.

Other contacts I had with Mary Robinson were slight enough – mostly through the Irish Association and also when we shared a platform at a meeting in the Clarence Hotel chaired by the late Jim Kemmy and organised by his Democratic Socialist Party which debated the Anglo-Irish Agreement. (No prizes for guessing who came off best that night!) So I was terribly pleased when, at the start of her Presidential campaign, she telephoned me with a request that I would join her team as adviser on Northern Ireland. But, on further reflection, I found I just could not campaign against Austin Currie – not because he was Fine Gael but because of all that he and, in particular, his wife had endured in the North. So I very regretfully wrote to Mary explaining my dilemma. I think it was typical of her that, in her reply, she admitted to sharing something of the same sentiment herself. We can all be thankful now that she did not succumb to that feeling but went on to conduct a brilliant and compassionate Presidency which has won her admiration around the world. (I only know Austin Currie very slightly and have never met his wife).

I had always admired Mary and was delighted when, in Mount Anville, Mother Stephenson had said that Iseult reminded her of 'Mary Bourke'. I had tramped behind Mary at Woodquay, finding unexpected tears in my eyes when gazing down at the relics of wattle and fences and heaps of mussel-shells placed there by my Viking (Ní Uigínn) ancestors. As UN Commissioner for Human Rights may she light a large candle for the whole world!

As I mentioned earlier, I knew our present President, Mary McAleese, when we were members of Seán MacBride's Enquiry into the Penal System. I had first heard her speak, in black leather trousers and white satin blouse, to a Meeting of the Irish Council for Civil Liberties in North Frederick Street and later was also very glad to hear her at a Summerfest in Corrymeela where she partnered Rev. Ruth Patterson (of the Presbyterian Church). It seems to me that Mary McAleese's fidelity to meditation is bringing many blessings on her work and on us all and I am proud of her Presidency. The work of another candidate for that Presidency, Adi Roche, is stunning too, isn't it?

WONDERS

Yes, it is true
the less well-off
know more about reality
than others do
whom money shelters
but all the same
I've seen amazing things
my forebears never dreamed of.

I've seen a pope
go pilgrimming to Canterbury
and I've felt the scald of sudden tears
when cardinal red
first coloured
Belfast's long grey Anglican Cathedral.
I've proudly watched
two mothers of young children
inspect a Presidential guard-of-honour
at what was first
the residence of the Viceroy
and I've heard a wailing didgeridoo
call back across the endless years of dreaming
and of mysterious inheritance,
binding the then with what we know as now,
focusing thought on You, the fount of all our being
whom I have been privileged to share
as Eucharistic minister.

CHAPTER THIRTEEN

'In Dublin's Fair City ...'

Before my involvement in the peace movement in the early seventies, I had been roped in by Sheila Dundon to help in a meals-on-wheels group delivering dinners from Temple Street Hospital. The group had gathered to help Sister Leontia, who had originally trudged around the area herself with a basket on her arm into which she had packed a number of hot dinners spooned into used plastic containers. Some of the people whom we served with dinners at that time were living in conditions that had to be seen to be believed – living was hardly the word for it; they were barely eking out an existence in tenement houses such as those which my Sullivan and Healy forebears had been so proud to possess in the once fashionable Mountjoy Square. You might find a little old lady all alone in such a derelict place where the rats were competing with the developers for a take-over. By degrees a better system for the dinners gradually became established and the plastic containers were replaced by charcoal-heated hot-locks, supplied by the Eastern Health Board, who eventually became involved also with the overall problems of those we served with dinners.

But I remember how helpless we had felt in our early years as to how to stitch such people into the bureaucracy of the Health Service. There did not seem to be a Public Health Nurse to call on and the Medical Social Workers and the religious communities of the hospitals from which we brought meals were unable to take on the problems of the district as well. Yet the problems we encountered were considerable. I once wrote an impassioned account of some of them for an unsuspecting Minister for Health who, with his wife, had kindly invited Eoin and me to luncheon at their home in another connection. I instanced a man living not in a room but in what had been the window-less coal-hole of a Mountjoy Square mansion, the sort where a lid got lifted in the pavement above and the coal had been thrown down. I told of an elderly, lame former dressmaker in Eccles Street alone in a five-storey house whom it was difficult to reach because the floor-boards in the hall and stairs had almost given way and the banisters had been used for firewood. I spoke of a grandmother, beaten up by her grandson for the few shillings in her gas meter, whom I had found on her floor with broken ribs and whom I had not been able to get into any hospital. (Eventually, a nursing nun had agreed to turn a blind eye to their rule of not going out of her own district and had attended to the old woman because the case was so pitiable). I talked of my malaise about how sometimes patients might be discharged from hospital once it was learned that they were receiving our dinners (five days a week), even though they might be living in situations where they could call on no other form of assistance whatever. I told of a man, much too ill to eat our food, who remained on the list in the hopes that his son might eat the dinner instead. But his unfortunate son was only interested in drinking large mugfuls of 'Amicardo – the Irish sherry' which at that time could be purchased at ten shillings per bottle. What I thought the Minister could do about these and many other problems I don't know, but I found it a mighty worrying thing to be put on notice of the difficulties of such people and often to have nobody with whom to discuss them other than a kindly chef in the kitchens to which we returned the empty dishes. From Temple Street some of us moved on to St. Brendan's Hospital and later to the Mater Hospital to get more services going. From the Mater one or two helpers started other new services from hotel kitchens on the Airport Road, while Sister Frances Dolores of the nearby convent of the Irish Sisters of Charity subsequently established a caring service in the district for those on the Dinners List from the Mater. This was an enormous relief; it is a nasty feeling to realise that one is developing a trick of edging towards the door of someone in real need of attention while saying cheerfully: 'Eat that up now, Mr. Byrne, while it's hot!'

Another part of Dublin life which I had come briefly to experience when our children were younger was to do with the Juvenile Court. The bicycle of one of our boys had been stolen from his school by some young people out on the tear from the inner city. Our boy was young and was required in court to identify his bike so I went along, only to be riven to the heart by the desolate wail of another mother whose son was driven away from there to serve a sentence in Letterfrack for stealing that bicycle. It was not a pretty story, the history of that day out, and unfortunately, it had culminated with a knife attack on a small girl who had tried to save her pet hen from the bunch, receiving cuts on her hands as a result. But some of the day had been innocent enough, collecting cakes unwanted by Johnston Mooneys and visiting the Zoo. Anyway, here was this mother standing up in court and more or less screaming while, straightaway her child was driven into Connemara where she had no hope of seeing him for over a year. When we caught up with one or two of those lads at a later stage after their time in Letterfrack, they were knowledgeable about such things as that milk came out of cows and not out of bottles; whether, however, the disappearance of some tennis racquets from a club from which they had been seen departing had anything to do with them I wouldn't know. What I DO know is that it seemed to take a large garden, the nearby Phoenix Park, tennis courts, swimming clubs, football matches, riding lessons and God knows what else to provide our own boys with sufficient outlets for their energies. What inner city boys in flats, with maybe a balcony if they were lucky, were supposed to do to amuse themselves I could not say and I thought ruefully how the gardens of many houses in say Seán McDermott Street had been turned into carparks for such as myself when we wanted to frequent the Gresham and nearby attractions.

It was when I was driving out to Clontarf one evening at the invitation of the Ladies Club there to talk about 'Peace in Northern Ireland' that at least one aspect of the anomaly of the situation hit me. By mistake I had turned down Summerhill where 'Handbag Corner' had become notorious and where I thought the lights would never turn to green to let me through. So when the discussion with the Clontarf ladies turned to 'what can WE do for peace?', I found myself remarking that as well as regretting the no-go areas in the North, perhaps we might have to take a look at some of those around our own city – where the divisions mainly between the haves and the have-nots were deepening all the time. Something a little similar happened to me more recently when a group on the northside of Dublin asked me to speak about the latest document published by the 'Faith and Politics' group. The invitation came from a teacher working in a not very affluent area who warned me not to get off the DART at that station but to go on to the next, where she would meet me and drive me back. We were half-way through our meeting when a boy put his head around the door to alert this hard-working, devoted teacher and mother to the fact that her small car had been broken into. 'There go the biscuits for our tea afterwards', she smiled apologetically but went on to add: 'Perhaps they needed them more than we do!'

It was in the early seventies that Judy Hayes drew the attention of 'Working for Peace' to the threatening situation then developing in Benburb Street where protesters had taken over the street and had even mentioned placing IRA sharpshooters on the rooftops. With some difficulty we managed to arrange in Leinster House an all-party meeting where the elected representatives of that area would sit down together with these constituents and discuss their current problems. (It seemed that few, if any, of their deputies had previously been in touch with them until we stuck our necks out and more or less insisted). I remember bringing the spokespeople of the protesters to Leinster House for the meeting and sitting with them in the waiting-room on the right of the main hall until they were collected and ushered upstairs. That room is not very large but they were almost overwhelmed by its proportions: 'We've never been anywhere like this before', they marvelled.

I think it was soon after this disturbance that Father Michael Sweetman S.J. and some companions took up residence in Benburb Street and later in Ballymun; Michael bringing with him compassion and that gentle but forthright courage which was his charisma. At Glencree we were glad indeed of his participation and of his chairmanship of the project for some time.

THE STRIKE (Dublin Corporation workers, 1968)

Lovely the laughing children on the strand
all brown and merry making castles gay
or catching scuttling crab with daring hand!
But some have piles of rubbish for their play.

Fresh and enlivening the salty sea
and calming to the soul its mighty swell
but those who most have need of holiday
are city-bound and festering in its smell.

Our well-fed offspring battle with their foes
on tidy tennis-court or swimming-pool
while happy parents feel they've done their best
to fit them for another year at school.

Surely *we're* not to blame for others' woes?
Not *our* responsibility the choking drains?
So pressing costly perfume to our nose,
levites! – we think about our 'capital gains'.

CHAPTER FOURTEEN

'Meanwhile back at the ranch ...'

Alongside all of this let me briefly try to sketch Eoin's career. When we were young and our children were having school holidays in what had been his parents house in Salthill, Galway, where life seemed so much simpler and easier to manage – not least because my mother-in-law's former housekeeper, Mrs. Hanberry, used to come in daily and do everything possible to assist us – I dreamed of how lovely it would be if we lived full-time in Galway. So it was not (contrary to some Galway opinion) Eoin's Dublin wife who had discouraged him from applying for the Professorship of Surgery in UCG which became vacant on the retirement of his father. Instead, before long, he was appointed to that position in University College, Dublin. 'I don't want my Daddy to be a "perfessor"', said a cautious Kevin (himself now a consultant surgeon in the Mater). 'I just want him to be my Daddy'.

Quite.

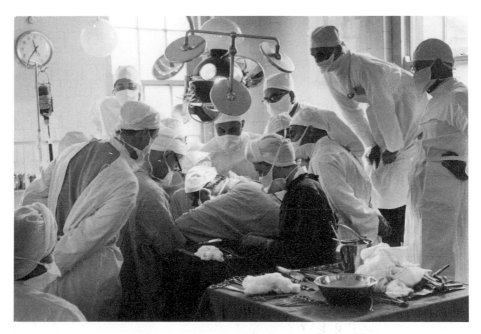

At my most testy I would mutter that I was not so much concerned about the issue of celibacy of clergy but about the families of surgeons and at times I would see myself as a single parent. It fascinated me, moreover, that although it was invariably I who went to the parent/teacher meetings at Belvedere, the boys' reports were only addressed to their father. (A bit like the Bishop of Galway who, although he had conducted our wedding, still only addressed his Christmas cards to Eoin). But in that same way as I believed that I would have to take on causes other than my own children, whenever I came face to face with results of Eoin's work I would have to stop grumbling and to thank God for it.

A good example would be at a swimming gala where I was cheering loudly for Eoin Jr. – then a medal-winning competitor – when the woman beside me asked me if he were my son and whether his father by the same name was a surgeon. It turned out that her own son, in lane five, had been a patient of Eoin's, a boy who, at that time, could not even walk. A successful heart operation had now brought him into competition with all of his age group. 'He won't win today', said his mother happily, 'but he'll be able to go home to his brothers and talk about the way things went instead of never being able to take part in anything'. After that, somewhat misty-eyed, I switched my allegiance and cheered for lane five instead.

At one time Eoin operated in 'The Cedars' Hospital in Dun Laoghaire – now the National Rehabilitation Centre. The changeover from a chest hospital became necessary, said the then Reverend Mother to me, 'because Mr. O'Malley operated on all our patients who then got better and went home leaving the wards empty'. (She must never have heard of Dr. Noel Browne!). He also worked in St. Luke's in Rathgar and the National Maternity Hospital, as well as the Mater Hospital. When it was decided to open a cardiac unit in the Mater, he undertook the work there in the first instance. To prepare for this he spent some time with Mr. Bill Cleland at the Postgraduate Hospital in Hammersmith in London and with Dr. Frank Gerbode in the Presbyterian Hospital in San Francisco. I remember visits to the Irish Club in London to be with him there for a few days at a time and to Pacific Heights in San Francisco where my cousin Mary Lou Schofield and I stayed for a couple of weeks. In Dublin I refrained from commenting much about trial operations on broken-down greyhounds and received blood-stained vests worn at the Veterinary College, for laundering, without much enquiry, and I would say to animal rights protesters: 'If YOU were the parent of the boy in lane five and you had to choose between a wheel-chair for your son and one of those dogs, which would you choose?' Animals do have rights for sure, but then so have people.

Eoin also served on such bodies as the Higher Education Authority and Comhairle na nOspidéal as well as the Board of the Mater Hospital. He was a member, also, of the Council of the College of Surgeons and was its President in the momentous years 1984–1986 when the College celebrated its bicentenary. How he managed to combine all this with a busy practice I don't know but somehow he did. In conjunction with the bicentenary celebrations we made trips to England, Scotland, Australasia, and America where he was conferred with Honorary Fellowships by the Colleges there. The Charter Day dinner in our own college that year was a gala affair for which I managed to find a gown which, if it was not exactly the style of two hundred years ago, still looked suitably antique and was accordingly admired. I like to remember that it was after that celebration that the college finally put its previous arrangements for women guests behind it. (I draw a veil over the rules made for lady diners prior to then). Some customs can be slow to change but not all precedents are worthy of retention!

178

Sometimes my participation in the peace movement presented unexpected difficulties, such as the time when Ronald and Nancy Reagan visited Dublin and were either welcomed enthusiastically or protested against vehemently, not only by some of my friends but by some of my own family. Nancy Reagan, step-daughter of a distinguished American surgeon, Loyal Davis, was warmly welcomed to the Royal College of Surgeons in Ireland by its then President, Eoin O'Malley, its Council and staff, where she presented a portrait of Dr. Davis – an Honorary Fellow of that college.

After that reception, Eoin and I were among the guests invited by the Reagans to lunch at the US Embassy in the Phoenix Park. But I, like most members of the peace movement at that time, was in knots about the American performance in Nicaragua and I felt slow to become involved in the celebrations unless I could first put down some small marker of dissent from such policies. My problem was resolved by a friendly Counsellor in the US Embassy who undertook to pass on beforehand my written protest to a close aide of the President and so I felt comfortable to attend, but wearing just a very plain white cotton suit with my black-and-white 'What Price Peace?' badge featuring its black cross. 'I like your brooch, Una', twinkled Seán Donlon, Secretary of the Department of Foreign Affairs, across the lunch table. At the College of Surgeons the Vice-President's wife, Nuala Lane, stood in for me as hostess, but anyway America's First Lady was so surrounded, nobody would have noticed my half-hearted performance there.

For almost thirty years now Eoin and I have enjoyed a lakeside second home in the West, something which, I think, has kept us at least partly sane. A lake is a mystical companion, forever changing, never in the same mood for long, yet always willing to share and to offer itself to you. The grounds around the bungalow and the care of the boat have been mostly managed by Eoin, but Paul Joyce and nowadays his son, Gerard, give valuable assistance, without which we could not cope. Moreover they are the most wonderful neighbours, always ready to help if there is trouble with straying cattle or to haul up or launch the boat. Mrs. Nancy McDonagh has minded the house and preserved it beautifully for us during all the years we have owned it, while Paraig Faherty and his team have faithfully maintained its structure. Nowadays, we enjoy lovely shrubs and trees in what was originally an almost bare site and we are joined by more and more birds whose songs in spring and summer are truly out of this world. You may see a young hare fastidiously nibbling your newly-seeded grass when you look out of the window or a fox or a stoat might take a short-cut through your heather while a pygmy shrew may scuttle across your car-port. But unless you stay up at night you won't catch Mr. Brock and his party as they sweep through on their traditional route, something established long before the houses were built. It would be nice if the badgers would replace their divots after them but that is not their way. Butterflies and dragonflies you will see galore and the surrounding spiders are agile beyond belief! The coveted mayfly may, in appropriate season, be bought nowadays from girls as well as from boys by the lake-shore but what does or does not happen when you finally get out on the lake with your flies would fill another book, which I am not competent to write. And while we are enjoying all this Ruth Doherty and her husband John keep an eye on our Dublin flat and send us our post.

By far the most unusual journey which Eoin and I have
made together was to the Sudan where we travelled in 1980
with our friends, Mac and Maeve McAuliffe Curtin as guests
of the regime there. This was my only visit to Africa and it was
indeed memorable. A number of Sudanese medical students
were at that time training in Dublin and Irish consultants were
invited to their country to repay hospitality and to advise
further. Nothing stays in my mind more than the cheerfulness
and equanimity of the people, their warm welcome, and their
extraordinary stoicism as patients suffering from conditions
such as bilharzia and medura foot. If ever I saw dignity I saw it
there – a dignity which required neither possessions nor
comforts to make its presence felt. After some days in
Khartoum we travelled south, stopping overnight at Wad
Medani before reaching Dinder. Our transport was an open-
topped jeep driven by a young Muslim who would faithfully
take out his prayer-mat and pray at stated intervals along the

way. I was very glad that he did because I didn't see how else he would find his way across the vast unmarked desert and once when the jeep turned over sideways in soft sand it must have been the power of prayer that pulled us out and got us straightened up again. Also I was rather nervous of the large barrel of petrol placed beside me in the back; what if it got overheated in the blazing sun? But all went well and we finally arrived at our huts made of fresh straw where at night we could hear lions roaring quite close by. Maybe being so vocal at night made them sleepy by day; at least whenever we saw them they seemed a bit weary but fleet-footed herds of giraffes and antelope treated us to their beautiful ballets with stunning effect. In the middle of the bush, for no reason that was clear to us, we were led to a large marquee in which lots of men were standing around in their dignified long white tunics while others, seated at rather antique Singer sewing-machines, were running up more of the same. Perhaps our driver or minder was calling for a new number he had ordered – at all events it was an amazing sight to come upon in the middle of what seemed to be pure forest.

Returning to Khartoum after a few days we did not recross the desert by jeep but instead flew back in 'Taxi Joey'. This was a five-seater plane, not complete with cocktail cabinet like the private one in which Tony O'Reilly had once given me a lift, but a small plane nevertheless with an Ethiopian pilot who got us safely back to our destination. Mind you, that was a relief because, as we boarded the aircraft in a clearing in the bush we couldn't help noticing the wreckage of a similar vehicle perched in the trees above our heads. Somebody said that it had been there for a couple of years but we refrained from asking further questions since we were keen not to distract the pilot nor to appear impolite.

As parents we have been glad to watch our children develop – some assisted by wives who have turned them into better husbands and fathers than, perhaps, we had a right to expect. One of our major surprises was when, out of the blue, Chris became a Member of the European Parliament. I had the pleasure of breaking the news to him one day (when he came in from Belfield in the inevitable frayed jeans) that Fine Gael Headquarters had phoned to say that Richie Ryan was moving to the Court of Auditors and now he, Chris, was to take his seat in the Parliament! At that stage Chris was twenty-seven years of age and was completing a Masters degree. True, he had been voted top of the replacements list by the Party (he had been leader of Young Fine Gael) but the chances of a replacement being needed were so remote as never to be considered further. For me it was a doubly emotional experience to hear him speak in Strasbourg, where he and Aideen Hayden, his wife, showed us around, because my father in his day had set much store by the young League of Nations in Geneva and had believed in the importance of nations coming together in the interests of peace. Obviously from his letters at that time he had had few illusions about the machinations behind the scenes and also about the sheer boredom of much that takes place in such bodies but, nevertheless, I felt sure he would be proud of a grandson – for a time the youngest member of that parliament – representing Dublin in a Europe not long recovered from a second world war.

Subsequently we have come to know something of Luxembourg where Art and his wife – Margie Waters, with their two children – had their base. Eoin Jr., after taking a doctorate in Sussex University, has worked always in Dublin in the ESRI, while Kevin, after surgical training in a number of different centres is, with his wife Annemarie Linehan and their four children, once more a resident of Dublin. Finbarr and Iseult are lawyers. I sometimes wonder when Tom O'Higgins, looking into the middle distance, had said he thought that perhaps the O'Malleys favoured the Labour Party, whether with some sort of second sight he was missing out a generation and was seeing instead that almost all of Eoin's and my children would do just that. (Chris has joined the Labour Party since serving as a Fine Gael MEP). We welcomed Finbarr's appointment as legal adviser to the leader of the Labour Party and Tánaiste, Dick Spring, from 1992–1997, and afterwards to the Labour Party under Ruairí Quinn's leadership. Iseult's involvement with FLAC, her chairing the Refugee Agency, and her serving on the Hepatitis C Tribunal (Tribunal of Inquiry into the BTSB) have been impressive, not to mention her appearances on 'Questions and Answers'.

We now have eight grandchildren to encourage and develop us and occasionally to draw demarcation lines for us as to where their space begins and ours ends. 'You're not the boss of me', a five-year-old assured me but, since she was the same lady who had previously enquired whether I thought she might grow up to be beautiful like my mother, I couldn't be cross for long. And, of course, she was right – I'm NOT the boss of her (thank God) but was she too young, I wonder, to take in anything of what I managed to say in reply (rather to my surprise): 'That's right', I said, 'only YOU are really the boss of you and only you can make yourself be good and grow up well'.

It's a fine art, isn't it, learning how to relate to children? Sometimes I think I have passed over a lot of their wisdom without attending to it properly. I think of one day when I was struggling to write a paper on Reconciliation and feeling a little testy because some of the neighbouring children were making a distracting noise. This was when we were in 'Dunamase' and there was a sort of no-one's-land between us and the new houses in the course of being built, on which some young boys had developed a kind of den. That afternoon a row had broken out between them and soon a tearful 'I don't want to play with you anymore' was followed by sounds of noisy departures. There followed silence. Than a sage spoke: 'Let's go and tell them we're sorry', said he, 'because maybe we DID something wrong and anyway it won't be any fun without them'. So the reconciliation mission departed the camp to return before long with the rest of the company. It had been well worth my while to pause in my writing efforts to pick up on a real-life example of how a peaceful society can be developed ...

Because, as I have said in my introduction, women have been so frequently written out of history and also because so few of the stories in this book could have happened without a lot of help, I list now at least some of the names of those who helped to keep our show on the road at different times. I do this also because, while it is said that behind every good man there is a good woman, certainly behind a woman like me there were lots of good women picking up the pieces. So I pay thankful tribute to, amongst others:

Silver-haired Mrs. Rose Swan, who lovingly could put children to bed and then whip up a hot chocolate soufflé for our dinner while cheerfully singing 'Daily, daily, sing to Mary!' – before hopping on the back of her son-in-law's motor-bike to zoom off home.

Marvellous Mrs. Mulally who made apple tarts daily for the 'holy horrors' (our children) coming home from school and whose face in death wore the same sweet smile she had always given to us in life.

Mrs. Keegan and her daughter, Brideen, who left everything fresh and sparkling after their visits and with whom our children would happily go to Herbert Park on walks. Miss McCarthy from Fairview, who had never crossed the Liffey until her breadman had assured her she would like the southside, since there were nice broad roads there as well.

Lots of children's nurses – some trained, as I have said, in Fairy Hill (Anne Ivory was our first), some in Temple Hill. I think of one girl, possibly the best of them all, whose parents arrived unannounced on the doorstep and removed her forthwith because they did not approve of her Dublin boyfriend and another (who rode a large motor-bike) from Stamullen. Others did not have badges or certificates, but had lots of commitment and fondness for children.

Au pair girls came mostly from Switzerland, encouraged by Una Wolf in Weggis; Una, whose parents had been neighbours of my grandmother and my mother in Dundrum. Two Brigittes from there were of enormous assistance. I still think of Briggie Mark 1 attempting to dislodge a herd of twelve steaming black cows who in a deluge of rain had taken up a stand on our lawn instead of proceeding to the Phoenix Park, as intended. 'Tauro, tauro', challenged Briggie as she flapped a red tablecloth hopefully at them. She enjoyed Dublin so much that she stayed with us a second year and studied stained glass at the Harry Clarke studio.

In the West I think of Mrs. Nancy McDonagh, whom I have already mentioned, and Mrs Kathleen Hanberry who, when she heard we were moving to a house called 'White Lodge' said to the boys out of hard-earned experience: 'Well it'll be "Grey Lodge" when ye get into it!'

I should mention also the very helpful men who made life easier for us – gardeners, delivery-men who would carry in the groceries and leave them on the kitchen table for you, not to mention an elderly milkman from the Hillcourt Dairy who would put the milk bottles into the fridge in case the tits wanted to treat themselves to it at the doorstep. And, I'm ashamed to say that in all the years I was in 'Dunamase' I never discovered where our butcher was actually located. When we moved in there originally there was a fair amount of work to be done in the house so I turned to the *Golden Pages* looking for people who would deliver while I was housebound. Ten years later I was still working the same system since Mr. Kevin Healy was sending us just what I wanted and his assistant, another O'Malley, would come smilingly not only with our order but with whatever cash I needed as well! As for Johnston Mooney's breadman, we all loved to see his van draw up and to choose from his rows of buns and small cakes, while a greengrocer called twice weekly with fresh vegetables and fruit. After my mother's death dear Maeve Marnan would often lend me her cheerful encouragement, affection and invaluable services in a way that I found most comforting and which retained for me the link with 'Carraig Breac' and her visits there. She was a favourite too with all the family, taking a particular interest in each one's pursuits. Dear 'Marnie' has died in England; heaven will be the better for her coming.

As for hobbies – I had always loved to sing since I can first remember. As a child at Christmas I greatly enjoyed the pantomimes and perhaps the one I liked best was that put on in the Father Mathew Hall in Church Street where afterwards the priests would invite us backstage to meet some of the cast. I am nearly sure I first saw Maureen Potter there when she was very young playing in 'Babes in the Wood'. Later I greatly enjoyed the Belvedere Operas – little thinking that one day I would have five boys of my own in that school! Old Belvedere and the Rathmines and Rathgar Society also put on musical shows in which Maria Vianni and Louise Studley and others would charm the birds off the bushes. (Later our own Chris proved a very attractive soprano lead in a Belvedere musical, looking and sounding every inch a princess).

I was married and had two children when I took myself to Michael O'Higgins (no relation) for singing lessons. Later, when he was on the staff of the R.I.A.M., I was a member of his group 'The Thirteens' where I was introduced to music like Fauré's 'Requiem' and Mozart's 'A Minor Mass' in which my neighbour, Nuala Staines, sang the soprano part as beautifully, it seemed to me, as Kiri te Kanawa. After Michael O'Higgins retired I had the great good fortune to be further encouraged by Eily O'Grady and her husband Frank Patterson, real friends to us all. Through Frank's good offices I became a member of Dr. Hans Waldemar Rosen's Radio Eireann Choral Society and rejoiced in swelling the chorus which sang with Seán O'Riada in the Gaiety and in being part of many concerts such as Wagner's 'Meistersingers' under the baton of Dr. Albert Rosen.

But sadly my choral practices had to give way to 'peace meetings' eventually (as did my stints with meals-on-wheels). When I explained this to Dr. Rosen he was very understanding and sympathetic because the North by then was in agony while, in the South too many preferred to believe that everything was happening 'up there' and that all we could do was to pray or sigh about it.

In recent years, since retiring from active participation in the peace movement, I have encouraged myself to write and so have taken part in most enjoyable writers' groups with Dorothy Carpenter, Pat Schneider, and later with Susan Byrne. Rather to my surprise I have found that some of my writing comes out in what I like to think are poems but my struggles with my lap-top and, before that, my word-processor are best not reported on! (Isn't that so, Finbarr?)

A MAN FROM HOPE

'There must be words for this' I thought
but none would come
though Goldsmith and Edmund Burke gazed on
and Thomas Davis decked with stars and stripes
and Grattan 'gainst whose plinth I eased my back,
fine wordsmiths all, but language I had none
fit for the wonder of that winter day.
Sun on the columns of the House of Lords,
on lion and unicorn keeping ancient watch
to rival latter-day security, while all the cameras of the world
looked on. But still no words would come
to liberate the meaning to my mind

until at last there rose one mighty roar
and words no longer mattered save these four;
A MAN FROM HOPE

– College Green, Dublin, 1 December 1995

190

WILLIAM JEFFERSON CLINTON

3/24/2001

Dear Mrs,

Sean O'Huiginn got your
lovely poem written on the
occasion of my first trip to Ireland
to me.

Thank you, your lines lifted
my spirits and warmed the cold
New York weather.

I hope to meet you when
I come back to Ireland —

Sincerely,

Bill Clinton

AFTERWORD – *or*
THE GRAND CANYON SYNDROME

I realise, of course, that, throughout, my perspective of 'peace' seems to favour retention of the Union with Britain and also that I can be accused of lacking sympathy for and understanding of the Nationalist position. If this is true I think that it is mostly the cruelty of the IRA which has so fashioned me. I see Loyalist savagery as being mainly a response to the IRA but, more specifically, I see the IRA as somehow imagining that they are acting on behalf of people like myself. Consequently, I have felt called upon to lean against them as much as possible and to lean towards those who are, in the end of the day, a minority on the island. This does not mean, however, that I am devoid of sympathy for and even of some understanding of INDIVIDUALS caught up in militant Republicanism. One Christmas I sat with a member of Sinn Féin in a Dublin hotel where a small shiver took hold of me when he said he wondered whether he would see the next Christmas. Beside us a decorated tree sparkled with lights, happy people were embracing each other and exchanging gifts while carols supplied background melodies. And here was this comparatively young man living out his form of moderation on the edge. Moreover, an unresearched part of me even wants to have more respect for such a compatriot than for the happy-gang who tell the likes of me that we're 'great to be so involved', who are very keen to follow developments on radio or television so as to be able to discuss them, but for whom the other side of the street is infinitely preferable when it comes to making a stand. But fortunately I have never been in a sufficiently important position where it would really be of consequence if I developed such feelings further and so instead I just continue with what I have come to call my 'Grand Canyon' syndrome. This refers to a time when the pilot of an aircraft in which I was a passenger announced that we were about to fly over the Grand Canyon on our right and, with that, almost everyone on board that jumbo jet stood up and hurried across to the right to look out. All except me, I think, who somehow had the idea that if I went over to the left I could single-handedly keep that plane balanced!

Maybe working for peace has to be a little like that, trying to listen to those who, if they were not exactly voiceless, still have less of a listenership than others around you might enjoy. But my main antipathy towards the IRA is that I have no wish to be in any way identified with the sort of United Ireland they seek to deliver to me. Unity of hearts and minds comes a long way before political unity in my book.

To conclude, I must sincerely thank you if you have journeyed with me this far and have listened to my story. You have done me an immense service. May you, in turn, discover someone who will sit down and listen to *you* for, while it is true that 'it is in giving that we receive', is it not also true that in receiving we can give? Certainly a large contribution towards building a peaceful community is to find enough time and space in which to listen to others, getting to know something of their real story – particularly others who may have upset and offended you.

Twentieth Century Revisited

It isn't comfortable to be revisionist
stare into the eyes of a lost leader
while questioning his values,
take down the busts of heroes from their columns
and lose them in the attics of the memory,
remove their pictures from the walkways of the mind,
pass by their monuments. But it may be
that they were premature in their ambitions;
and when the blood was young and hot, with pulses racing,
they undertook a war of separation
which might have been avoided. Maybe this blood-stained
    century
now should be granted leave of absence
or amnestied in mothballs,
and the indomitable Irishry of North and South
should gaze into the faces of their children
and not their ancestors
while planning for the future.

– Glannrowan, 1999

Appendices

LAST LETTER OF RORY O'CONNOR to his sister EILY

Mountjoy
8th December 1922

About 7 a.m.

Dear Sister Eily,

I have just finished a General Confession. I am going calmly to death with four dear comrades. Is it not the Grace of God that I am given time to confess and not like some others who have to answer the call without notice.

Dearest: You and all will mourn for me. DO NOT DO SO. Is it not a magnificent death?

I forgive all my enemies. I have never felt any feelings of revenge.

Were you aware that the devotion of my life has been to the Blessed Virgin and this day I had just finished a Novena in honour of the Immaculate Conception. The anniversary of my First Communion. God bless you and protect you all.

Your loving – if undemonstrative – brother,

Rory

(Kindly supplied by Rev. Michael O'Carroll C.S.Sp., Blackrock College)

In Liberating Memory*

Enda McDonagh

'Bear in mind these dead' was the simple and austere demand of the late John Hewitt. He dared 'not risk using that loaded word, Remember' and

> cannot urge or beg you
> to pray for anyone or anything
> for prayer in this green island
> is tarnished with stale breath
> worn smooth and characterless
> as an old flagstone, trafficked
> with journey's no longer credible to lost destinations.

Daunted by the 'savage complications of our past' (his own phrase) Hewitt confronted us with the dangers of Irish remembering. Our memorials like our monuments so easily weigh us down. We become the burden of our history. 'History may be servitude' (T. S. Eliot) but it may also be 'freedom'.

> This is the use of memory:
> For liberation – not less of love but expanding
> Of love beyond desire, and so liberation
> From the future as well as the past.

While we bear in mind these dead, Kevin Higgins, Tim Coughlan, Archie Doyle and Bill Gannon, we seek to do so in a liberating rather than enslaving spirit, the spirit which animates the readings from Ezechiel (36:22–28), Paul (1 Cor 11:23–26) and Matthew's account of Jesus' sermon on the Mount (Mt 5:38–48) which we have just heard.

The warnings of Ezekiel here and elsewhere are not far removed from those of Hewitt. Israel's profaning of Yahweh's name, a common cause for prophetic criticism, connects with stale breath and incredible journeys to lost destination of Irish prayer. In the verses immediately preceding his account of the Eucharist, Paul is sharply critical of the Christian divisions, which mar such celebrations. Jesus' summons to love of enemies could hardly be more strongly put. Warning and summons are also promise. A new heart, a heart of flesh to replace the heart of stone will come with God's own spirit which in Ezechiel's later vision will transform the valley of dry bones. The perfect love by which the father loves and to which Christians are called by Jesus is promised and achieved for all in the forgiving and liberating death of Jesus. That is the liberating remembrance which, as Paul reminds his readers, is ours in the Eucharist. How far are we ready for the liberating memory? How far are we ready for the Eucharist?

SERVITUDE OR FREEDOM?

It can be so easy to march to Mass. In the Irish Catholic tradition it is the Mass that matters. And some of our best Masses, if one may use such language, are funeral Masses and memorial Masses. And yet we must always ask ourselves how far the memorial is, like the history, an expression of servitude or freedom? How far does it expand into love of enemies or contract and leave us isolated with our own? If you love only those who love you and salute only your brethren – in church as in market place!

We need to reflect again on what we do at Mass – on what we do in memory, in memory of Jesus first of all and then in memory of the four people whose names are put before us today and beyond that, in memory of all of our divided forebears. What we do at Mass, we do in symbol, in sign and sacrament, not in reduction of the reality but in enlargement of it. No Christian can put a boundary to the march and reach of the Mass, the reach of two hands extended on a cross, to embrace all people and especially those whose forgiveness he then prayed. That universal embracing provides our first memory. In memory of Jesus is obviously in imitation of Jesus, following Jesus as disciples to the point of taking up one's cross, of forgiving one's enemies, of embracing the whole world. Of course the memory and remembering go further. We are called and enabled not just to imitate Jesus, to behave like him but to be him, to enter into his forgiving death and resurrection, to share his life and love. In memory of him is a dying with him so that we may share the fullness of life which he embodies, the divine life of love itself. Not just *like* him but *him*. It is all way-out, fantastic, incredible like John Hewitt's journeys. And yet we eat the body and drink the blood. We are what we eat and drink, Christ. 'Worthily', as Paul reminds us, in the very next verses of I Corinthians, and 'worthily' in the earlier verses means not divided, not in factions, not the faction fighters for which we are so often criticised. 'And the first item on the agenda is a split': Brendan Behan on the Corinthians at Eucharist, on the Irish at Mass.

Do we dare do this in memory of Jesus and exclude strangers, opponents, enemies? And can we truly remember in Christ those who have gone divisively before us and fail to recognise their deeper present unity in Christ.

REPENT AND REPAIR

This divided island has much to repent and much to repair. The heritage of our history has been so much servitude as Gael and Gall; Irish, Scottish and English; catholic and Protestant have struggled to dominate and so enslave and so be enslaved. Our little memorial today is a tiny symbol of deeper Irish divisions, of wider human division from Belfast to Beirut to the Punjab, from Soweto to San Salvador. Can the arms on the cross stretch so far even for us who have grown up with its reconciling reach and pride ourselves, God bless the mark, on our fidelity in the footsteps, the agonising, broken footsteps of the Master on the via dolorosa, on our fidelity to the Mass? The haunting question remains, if we cannot celebrate this Mass, can we celebrate any Mass? Amos had a word about God's despising feasts and solemn assemblies and burnt offerings because of injustice, neglect, exclusiveness (Amos 5). Jesus picks up the same theme in his criticism of the Pharisees and in his injunction to his disciples to be reconciled before coming to make their offering (Mt 5:23f). For this we need expression, symbolic expression for that which is deepest in us, our sharing in Christ, his humanity and divinity, his death and resurrection.

'Will you speak to Tim on Resurrection Day?' What an arrogant and absurd question! We might ask it more often, particularly at our memorial and above all at our Mass. Ireland seems so crowded with people who proclaim oneness in Christ and look forward, at least in so far as their religious observance goes, to his coming again in fulfilment for all and yet who have such difficulty in greeting and accepting one another as Catholics or Christians or simple Irish. By this will they be known as disciples! By this will they be ready for Eucharist! The conventional obstacles to shared Eucharist between Christians of different denominations may sometimes be less formidable than those between Christians of one. Eucharist as task as well as gift may be as challenging to a group of Catholics as to a mixed group of Catholics and Protestants. This mass and any mass should challenge us deeply as any joint Eucharist between Catholics and Protestants. In he slow journey to mutual acceptance in Ireland, Eucharist should take its rightful place as a means as well as a goal of unity. If we were to await complete unity and acceptance among Christians, even Irish Catholics, Eucharist would forever recede. Such a concept of the Jesus' memorial would be a new form of servitude. The gift, for which we are always unready, is first of all gift and so carries its own readying and liberating force. Let us surrender to that liberating force today for ourselves and all the people on this island. It is I believe the final message of the four men we remember now folded in the single party of God.

> We cannot revive old factions
> We cannot restore old policies
> Or follow an antique dream
> These men, and those who opposed them
> And those whom they opposed
> Accept the constitution of silence
> And are folded in a single party.

And all shall be well and
All manner of thing shall be well
By the purification of the motive
In the ground of our beseeching.

(T. S. Eliot)

* Homily at a Memorial Mass for Kevin O'Higgins, Tim Coughlan, Archie Doyle and Bill Gannon, Church of the Assumption, Booterstown, Dublin, 11 July 1987. The Mass of Reconciliation marked the sixtieth anniversary of the assassination of Kevin O'Higgins, Minister for Justice in the Irish Free State, for which the other three men, all now dead, are believed to have been responsible. The Mass was arranged by Mrs Una O'Higgins O'Malley.

from 'The Politics of Forgiveness: A New Dynamic'

Haddon Willmer

(Originally published in *The Furrow*, April 1979. A full version of this article will be published in a future edition of *From Pardon and Protest*)

POLITICS AND FORGIVENESS

Bonhoeffer insisted in his *Ethics* that we must always begin with the reconciliation of God and the world of reality. They are not two separate spheres or two separate dimensions. The Christian (man in Christ or man being conformed with Christ) was as one whole man in the world because God and the world have been reconciled in Jesus Christ. Bonhoeffer believed Christian ethics to be a concrete ethic in which Christ takes form among us here and now. He then asked, pertinently, who is this 'us'? and what is our 'here and now'? … Our 'here and now' is historically conditioned, he argues, by our historical relations with Jesus Christ, whom we have been rejecting with disasterous historical consequences. Yet what we reject is our true self, our hope, as it were. Christ still waits in our here and now to take appropriate form among us. The appropriate form is taken among us especially in the Church, when it confesses as its sins, the sin of the world … He talks gladly of the word of forgiveness which is proclaimed and accepted and known as the ultimate reality in the Church. And parallel to that unqualified word of forgiveness as the free and full gift of God, there may be a healing of the wounds of past political guilt, so that even within the history of the internal and external political struggle of nations, there is something in the nature of forgiveness, though it be only a faint shadow of the forgiveness which Jesus Christ vouchsafes to faith in the Church. … Did Bonhoeffer's view of the relation of forgiveness and politics apply simply to those special circumstances, or was it of more general significance? Asking myself that question led me on the way to the politics of forgiveness.

ATONEMENT

My second route was not unconnected with the first. I shared teaching the doctrine of atonement with a colleague. I found that he sent students on to me well instructed in the early history of the doctrine and yet lacking an urgent and living sense that the great words and concepts we use to talk about the atonement were 'earthed', related to reality. I decided it was useless simply to go on historically from the point they had reached; so after some experiment, I started not by picking up the story in the sixteenth century but by pointing to something contemporary - the Holocaust. ... What makes such mass killing possible is in part our highly-organized technological society and its machinery. So the question is not merely to liberate or preserve men from suffering and death, but to find forgiveness of a humanity which is implicated in the guilt of creating and running these kinds of systems. In this perspective, we may begin to see that forgiveness is profoundly relevant to the very foundations of our existence and meaning as human beings in one human family today ...

I find the concept of forgiveness as continually elusive and mysterious as its practice is difficult and often painful. We need to clarify the word, but we also have to put up with some vagueness for some time yet, and perhaps always. As a contribution to such clarification let me try to identify some basic principles.

WHAT CANNOT BE CHANGED ...

First, what cannot be changed has to be forgiven. 'What cannot be changed' refers to things we cannot avoid, cannot abolish, cannot ignore. At least two things fall into this category. One is the past ... Forgiveness is not a magic to alter what has been done or to make the past other than it is. This is not to say that the past is a brute monolithic fact impervious to varying interpretation or prescribing a single future deterministically. It is to emphasize the real 'doneness' of the past - its awesome facticity. The other thing which cannot be changed and

therefore has to be forgiven is the other person or persons …
There is a certain unchangeability about the person and
persons in groups. They are hedged around by a certain
sacredness. I think the basic moral unchangeability of the
person is indicated by the commandment 'Thou shalt not kill'.
Of course you can kill. There is no great difficulty in killing
people and getting rid of them and I do not claim they are
unchangeable physically. It is a moral unchangeability, it is a
sort of sacredness - if you heed this commandment … then you
will recognize that persons cannot be abolished, pushed out of
the way or ignored. What cannot be abolished or ignored,
sooner or later has to be forgiven. I think we get driven to the
choice: either abolish and ignore, or forgive. Always of dealing
with the past or the person sooner or later present us with
pretty stark choices about either finding ways to forgive or else
being driven to try to get rid of the unchangeable and to justify
our violence. Forgiveness is such a curious concept.
Forgiveness is a response to what cannot be changed; it
respects that unchangeability yet finds a way of changing the
unchangeable. Forgiveness thus appears to be some sort of
event, act or spirit which human beings do find is somehow
given to them which changes the unchangeable by setting it in
a new context, shining upon it a light seemingly unthinkable,
even impossible. It is the unpredicatable power of new life and
new hope.

FORGIVENESS IN POLITICS

This brings me to my second point which is about the nature
of politics. It is very easy when we are realist to say, 'Politics is
a miserable business; forgiveness is quite foreign to it'. There
are certainly many styles of politics in which it is unnatural.
Therefore, when we come to look at politics with forgiveness
in mind, we tend to start thinking about where forgiveness is
needed, where there should be forgiveness in politics, but is
not, where we long for it and are left unsatisified. We focus on
the absence of forgiveness in politics … I think, however, that
we should look for the presence of forgiveness before we look
at its absence … I want to argue this general theory on the
grounds that operative forgiveness in politics is not a mere
ideal, but is a reality. The theory discloses what is the nature of
practical workable human politics … The politics of forgiving

205

is basic, because unless people did in fact forgive each other enough to make a moderately workable community, there would be no possibility of anyone having a community to exploit and use as a power for non-forgiving ends. So, forgiveness is a certain kind of natural power operative in politics.

When we are faced with the unforgivable, then it is necessary for man's sake to find the way of forgiveness. Forgiveness breaks out beyond the attempt to think that we can make people pay fairly for what they have done. The unforgivable drives us to break free from the feeling that we have got to revenge what has been done, because we realize that revenge is powerless in the face of the situation that has been brought about. ... Forgiveness is a word that fits this sort of problem. The problem demands that we break through to something better. At the same time, the breakthrough must take account of what has happened. Man cannot walk away from the atrocities of war as if nothing has happened. Just because there is no repair for Auschwitz and no adequate revenge does not mean it may be ignored. Forgiveness is a breaking through to the new which yet takes account of what has happened. It lives in conscious awareness of the baseline from which we operate - the baseline of a fallen world not of a perfectly good humanity. The past lives on - in forgiveness. So forgiveness is transformation rather than abolition of the past. Forgiveness is a rebuilding, a re-establishing of man, a re-affirmation even of the sinner and those caught up in his sin. ... Politics and forgiveness fit naturally together. We should not look for the gift of forgiveness in politics in the form of some decisive transition to a perfect society where forgiveness becomes unnecessary. We look not for the perfect society without offence, but for a society sustained by adequate forgiveness operating in persons and processes and institutions so that the offences that occur are deprived of their power to destroy the good fellowship of God and man. Such a society is not a ready-made divine gift out of the blue - it is a human, political ongoing task. There is such a thing as the political ministry of forgiveness.